The Franciscan Leader

A Modern Version of The Six Wings of the Seraph

An Anonymous Franciscan Treatise in the Tradition of St. Bonaventure

Translated by

Philip O'Mara

Franciscan Pathways

The Franciscan Leader

A Modern Version of The Six Wings of the Seraph

An Anonymous Franciscan Treatise
in the
Tradition of St. Bonaventure

Translated by

Philip O'Mara

Franciscan Pathways

The Franciscan Institute
St. Bonaventure University
St. Bonaventure, New York

This is a new and revised edition of
The Character of a Christian Leader, originally titled
The Six Wings of the Seraph by St. Bonaventure,
translated by Philip O'Mara. Ann Arbor, MI: Servant Books, 1978.

Scripture quotations are taken from The Revised Standard
Version Bible, copyrighted 1946, 1952, © 1971, 1973
by the Division of Christian Education of the
National Council of the Churches of Christ in the U.S.A.
and used by permission.

© 1997
Franciscan Institute Publications
St. Bonaventure University
St. Bonaventure, New York 14778

ISBN 1-57659-126-3

Printed at
BookMasters, Inc.
Mansfield, Ohio

Contents

	Preface	VII
	Introduction	XIII
	Prologue	1
One	The Need for Christian Leaders	3
Two	Zeal for Righteousness	7
Three	Brotherly Love	17
Four	Patience	23
Five	Good Example	31
Six	Good Judgment	37
Seven	Devotion to God	55
	Translator's Note	65

Preface

In the mid-1970s I was living in Ann Arbor, Michigan, and working as a researcher for various enterprises associated with the movement for charismatic renewal. Some of my work was in service to a large, mostly Catholic charismatic community, then called The Word of God, for which I directed a small pastoral reference library. Otherwise I did fact-checking, feature and review writing, and editorial work for the charismatic publishing house, Servant Books, and for the magazine, *New Covenant*, which circulated to prayer groups and communities all over the nation and beyond. Thanks to an undergraduate minor in Classics, and to frequent use of Latin sources in my years at Notre Dame, where I obtained a Ph.D. in English, I am a competent Latinist, and I was often asked to find references in the Fathers of the Church and in various medieval works of spirituality. Thus, when I was given an opportunity to translate a short treatise on monastic leadership, *De Sex Alis Seraphim*, from the Latin edition of the works of St. Bonaventure, I set to work with no misgivings. Soon, hoping to make sure that I would be faithful to the author's central ideas, I acquired offprints of a few articles on St. Bonaventure's style and spiritual teaching. Years before, I had used his longer *Life of St. Francis* for spiritual reading. (My middle name, taken in Confirmation, is Francis; it reflects a lifelong interest that has led to wide reading and some careful study.) I had met up with Bonaventurian materials from time to time in the course of literary research.

As I worked on the translation, however, I found to my dismay that neither the scholarly articles on St. Bonaventure, nor my recollections of his other works, nor my general knowledge of the Franciscan Order were of any help to me. Gradually I became convinced, for reasons that I eventually published in a separate article, that the treatise had not been intended for the Friars Minor at all, but for other religious communities. That article, which required wide-ranging research and which I did not finish for several years, is reprinted in this book. I need only admit here that, as I continued my work on the translation, it came as a complete surprise to learn that the Franciscan family, as far back as the last years of the thirteenth century, already included not only friars, cloistered nuns, and secular tertiaries but also tertiaries living a common life and professing religious vows. I wrote a memorandum to the editorial board, suggesting that we include a statement to the effect that the treatise had apparently been intended for members of the Third Order Regular, not for the Franciscan Friars. It was decided, however, that an edition principally intended to help lay leaders of charismatic prayer groups did not need to be burdened with a discussion of this question.

The translation went through several changes, and I am grateful still for the long, hard work of my editor, Nicholas Cavnar, and to the volunteer typist, the late Marga Picard, who helped me patiently through the many revisions that were needed. Then, on the very day when we went to press, as I checked a scholarly article on a completely different subject, I ran into a reference to Father Ignatius Brady's claim that St. Bonaventure had not written *De Sex Alis Seraphim* at all. Once I read Father Brady's arguments, I felt no more guilt about having missed all the Bonaventurian features of the book. I had been failing to see what wasn't there. Readers of the introductory article "Advice to Superiors," reprinted here with several small corrections, will see that, after a good deal of time in several libraries, I have been able, not to identify the priest who actually wrote this brief work, but to describe the circumstances and people for whom he wrote.

The author, who remains anonymous, was a fourteenth-century Franciscan priest, one who had studied St. Bernard and St. Bonaventure, one who had sharp eyes (and occasionally a downright cynical tongue) for folly and wrongdoing and lasting zeal for the kingdom of God. He believed that clear-sighted, strong leadership was entirely compatible with compassion for human frailty and with profound Christian piety. At a time when many lay Franciscans were adopting community life and when communities of Beghards and some others were affiliating with the Franciscans, he offered his treatise as a guide to effective leadership, Consequently, in a work designed to help religious superiors, he made no bones about the necessity, as he saw it, for the exercise of firm headship in religious communities. He had a clear awareness that deep spirituality is most real when it is most fully exercised in love of neighbor, and I soon found that when he used the term *pietas* as the name of the second Seraphic virtue of a leader (Chapter Three), his depiction of this virtue required me to translate the word, not as "piety" but as "brotherly love." In this translation I have tried to convey both his conviction that religious communities need vigorous direction and his awareness, demonstrated in his non-technical and varied terminology, that different circumstances call for flexibility in choosing the people responsible for such direction and in deciding on its scope. Ordinarily, I have adopted these translations for the author's vocabulary of leadership:

caput: head
custos: guardian (used only rarely, perhaps an isolated survival of the Friars' nomenclature)
magister: guide, director
praeesse: to direct, to govern
praelatus: leader, head
rector: guide, director
superior: guide
zelator: director

The original edition, prepared at a time when many Catholic charismatic groups were attracted to theories about strict leadership and when some groups were really infatuated with their own special terminology, made excessive use of the words "head" and "headship." The Latin original, as is shown above, uses several different words for leadership, and *caput* appears only when, in Chapter Five, no. 13, he makes use of St. Paul's analogy of the head and members of a human body. Most of his terms did not have narrowly defined applications in the religious groups of his age. He uses these terms almost interchangeably, so I have not felt obliged to find a single English term to translate the same Latin term in every instance. In general, however, I have preferred to translate his two favorite terms, *praelatus* and *rector*, as "leader" and "guide" respectively. Where "head" and "headship" read smoothly in context I have retained them, and in the one case where the author refers to the Pope as *caput totius Ecclesiae militantis,* I have translated this phrase as "head of the whole Church militant." He uses the word *magister* fairly often, but it is not easy to find, in his usage of this term, any nuances that would call for its translation as "master" or "teacher," so I have most often translated it as "guide."

The author of the treatise, writing in Latin, knew that his readers would be men, members, and chiefly leaders, of clerical communities. At times priests may have paraphrased or summarized the author's ideas for the assistance of Brothers or Sisters who could benefit from them, but the primary audience consisted of clergy. Today, many readers, women and men both, suffer genuine irritation when terms that relate only to men are constantly repeated in contexts where inclusive language is fully appropriate. If I were to change every passage where inclusive language could possibly be introduced, some sentences would be top-heavy with multiple uses of "him or her" and similar phrases, or I would have to replace singular with plural forms at the risk of making the author's ideas harder to grasp. This translation is chiefly intended to be useful for pastoral and spiritual purposes; scholarly precision is not aimed at, so I have solved this problem in various ways. I have borne in mind that the author wrote for communities whose superiors were priests, so I have usually retained male pronoun references for passages directly concerned with individual leadership. Where it is clear, however, that gender-inclusive language will not obscure any essential element in the author's teaching, I have tried to use language that avoids raising unnecessary barriers to the usefulness of the document. Sometimes I have used plural forms, sometimes I have relied on gender alternation, and sometimes, where the results of either change struck me as clumsy, I have retained the male-only terminology of the original.

The original edition omitted a few specifically Franciscan references: most of these have been restored in this revision, but I have not attempted to use the full allegory, in which each wing of the Seraph is identified with one of the virtues of leadership.

While I was working on this translation twenty years ago, Joan Hertzog and I began our married life together. In the early years of our marriage, while she was struggling to complete her own Ph.D. thesis in the somewhat remote field of Japanese Art History, she was a good listener and a helpful critic as I developed the ideas that went into my article on the Tertiary background of the treatise. Later, as our family increased through the adoption of two small children from Korea, she helped me to find time and quiet, even in the chaos that pre-schoolers bring to a home, for this work, just as I was happy to put it aside for family duties and to give her time for her own teaching and scholarship. Allow me to dedicate this book to my family: to Prof. Joan Hertzog O'Mara of Washington and Lee University and to our teenagers, Philip Joseph Martin Choi Joon Yung O'Mara and Caitlin Mary Ruth Song Mee Kyung O'Mara.

Philip F. O'Mara
Department of English
Bridgewater College
Bridgewater, Virginia

Introduction

Advice to Superiors in Early Tertiary Communities: De Sex Alis Seraphim [1]

Among the shorter works attributed to St. Bonaventure is found a study of the virtues of a religious superior, *De sex alis seraphim*, which has been used in religious communities ever since its initial publication at the end of the fifteenth century. Often reprinted, it has also been translated into German, French, and several times into English, and for generations was recommended especially in the Society of Jesus as a handbook for superiors.[2] The intrinsic qualities of the work had much to do with its popularity: its emphasis on practical moral psychology, its brief and memorable allegory, and what was considered its happy use of abundant scriptural references. St. Bonaventure's supposed authorship must have contributed to its high repute, all the more in that works on governance and pastoral care in the religious life were few; little existed apart from St. Bernard's treatise "On Precept and Dispensation." A book on leadership, presumably for the ministers and guardians of his own Order, by the Seraphic Doctor, who had himself been the Minister General, was surely to be prized; moreover its contents were general, its advice somewhat flexible and of wide application. Religious superiors of many institutes found it helpful and Claudius Aquaviva, the Father General of the

---

[1] This article was originally published in *Franciscan Studies* 48(1988): 81-104.
[2] The text is in Vol. 8 of St. Bonaventure's *Opera omnia* (Quaracchi, 1898), 131-51, with prefatory material on p. LX. The editors collated just one of the surviving manuscripts, of which only four were known, with the previous Vatican edition. There are translations by Fr. Sabinus Mollitor, O.F.M., *The Virtues of a Religious Superior* (St. Louis: Herder, 1920); Dominic Devas, *A Franciscan View of the Spiritual and Religious Life: Being Three Treatises from the Writings of St. Bonaventure* (London: Thomas Baker, 1922), 26-124; José de Vinck, "The Six Wings of the Seraph," *The Works of Bonaventure*, Vol. 3 (Paterson: St. Anthony Guild, 1966); and Philip F. O'Mara, *The Character of a Christian Leader* (Ann Arbor: Servant Books, 1978), reprinted with corrections and revisions in this volume.

Jesuits, could direct that Jesuit superiors were to study it, since "It is in conformity with our spirit and fits in with the Society's way of doing things."³

Ignatius Brady, O.F.M., has shown, however, that *De sex alis seraphim* is not by St. Bonaventure but is an anonymous fourteenth-century treatise.⁴ His three arguments against Bonaventurian authorship may be characterized respectively as weak, strong, and all but demonstrative. His weak argument is that there are no thirteenth-century manuscripts. Almost all European libraries have undergone such vicissitudes in seven centuries that in itself this reason is not telling, but it is not quite negligible, especially as not all the early manuscripts carry the traditional attribution. St. Bonaventure's confreres, had they supposed from the beginning that the treatise was his, might have been led to preserve the work in good early copies, especially when it would appeal by topic and treatment to heads of religious houses. All manuscripts, early and late, would be likely to carry St. Bonaventure's name. Much stronger, however, is the argument that the treatise, although it employs the same device of attributing specific meaning to the six wings of Francis's seraphic vision as is found in the Prologue to the *Itinerarium* and mentions the vision in terms consistent with its narration in *Legenda maior* (ch. 13), is stylistically quite different from these and all of St. Bonaventure's other authentic works. Brady's final argument is that this work employs certain terms that are not part of St. Bonaventure's vocabulary and that in fact date it to a period not earlier than the

---

³*Opera omnia*, 8: LX.
⁴"The Writings of St. Bonaventure regarding the Franciscan Order," *Miscellanea Francescana* 75 (1975): 89-112; this treatise is discussed on pp. 105-106. Fr. Brady's essay is reprinted in *San Bonaventura maestro di vita francescana e di sapienza cristiana* (Atti del Contresso internazionale per il vii centenario di San Bonaventura da Bagnoregio), ed. Alfonso Pompei (Rome: Pontificia facoltà Teologica San Bonaventura, 1976), with the same pagination. The book will hereafter be referred to as Pompei. Previous discussions of the *opusculum*, which have been few and brief, generally take the authorship of Bonaventure for granted; e.g., J. Guy Bougerol, O.F.M., *Introduction to the Works of Bonaventure*, trans. José de Vinck (Paterson: St. Anthony Guild Press, 1963) indicates the subjects treated, 161; dates and locates the work as composed at Orvieto, April, 1263, 174, and notes the popularity of the work among the Jesuits, 229. For a very brief discussion of essentially the same points, cf. Balduinus Distelbrink, *Bonaventurae scripta authentica dubia vel spuria critice recensita* (Roma: Istituto Storico Cappucini, 1975), 22. The author notes Fr. Brady's assignment of the *opusculum* to the list of incorrectly attributed works but does not discuss his reasons.

middle of the fourteenth century. He notes that "superior" and "rector" are used for the head of a religious house, a usage that did not occur in the thirteenth century, and that *praelatus* is used in a way not found in St. Bonaventure's time. This philological point virtually decides the question, and since the three arguments reinforce one another, together they may be taken as conclusive.

When the document is accepted as much later than the time of St. Bonaventure, other anomalies appear. This treatise on the virtues of a religious superior seems to avoid the ordinary Franciscan terminology and disregards some issues with which superiors in the Friars Minor would have to deal. The word minister never appears, and the sole occurrence of *custos*, in the phrase *custos animarum et rector* (guardian and guide of souls) (ch. 6:13), is non-technical. The author's chosen terms are *praelatus, rector, superior,* and at times *vicarius* and *magister,* all used interchangeably. *Monasterium* is preferred to *conventus,* and *locus,* in the sense of a small religious house, does not appear. Nothing is said of provincial government or of the relation of one house to another. References to preaching and to other external pastoral work are few and do not imply a community fully committed to the apostolate, nor is there mention of theological study. St. Francis is mentioned as founder (*patri nostro,* ch. 1:4), but the rules of the communities for which the author writes are not ascribed to him but are referred to as *a sanctis Patribus apte statuta* ("fittingly determined by our holy Fathers"), in the plural. There are some variations in these rules, it is observed, based on different views of what is expedient (ch. 2:7). Thus it seems likely that the author, himself a Franciscan, was not writing for the Friars Minor at all.

Other evidence supports this conclusion. When the author advises (ch. 6:20) that all major decisions be made in consultation with those directly affected, he situates his work in the Franciscan tradition, in which all the friars gathered for general chapters,[5] although this practice was abandoned even in Francis's lifetime. The discussions of disobedient religious are among the longest in the treatise (ch. 2:12-16; 6:8-9), but contain no suggestion that they be transferred to another house, an obvious possibility in a large

---

[5]John Moorman, *A History of the Franciscan Order From its Origins to the Year 1517* (Oxford: Clarendon Press, 1968), 28-29.

order. Rather, the stubbornly recalcitrant are to be expelled, without reference to the canonical difficulties derived from priesthood and solemn vows. There exists a peculiar anomaly in a summary of the main points of the treatise, attached as an addendum in the earliest edition and in one important manuscript (where it does not seem to be by the same hand but may be contemporary).[6] In the manuscript the discussion of the way to handle disobedient religious is entitled *de falsis fratribus, et qualiter sint removendi* ("On false brethren and how they are to be removed"). In the first printed edition, however, in defiance of the actual meaning and emphasis of the text, the reading of the title is changed to *tenendi* ("to be held on to").[7] Between the production of the manuscript, after the middle of the fourteenth century, and the first printed edition in 1495, it was realized that the text proposed to solve the problem in a way which, in a changed canonical situation, was no longer easy to achieve. But even in the fourteenth century a religious in solemn vows would not readily have been expelled and left to a worldly career. The celibate tertiary communities, ancestral to the Third Order Regular, for which, it will be argued here, *De sex alis seraphim* was written, did not obtain permission to take solemn vows until 1447; in the thirteenth and fourteenth centuries they consisted of persons sharing a common life, usually without vows.[8]

The author shows clearly that his essential spirituality is Franciscan. There are several references to life in union with Christ, especially in his Passion (ch. 5:9; 6:17; 7:6), and a reference to the "nakedness" of those who would be true disciples of Jesus (ch. 5:6). The repeated demand for fraternal correction of wrongdoers (e.g. ch. 5:7-10) is directly in the tradition of St. Francis, both as he is represented in official biography (Celano's *First Life*, ch. 76; *Second Life*, ch. 32-34, 39, 58, 66) and in legend (e.g. *Legend of Perugia*, 69-77). The warning against excessive use of books (ch.

---

[6] Quaracchi ed. 8: LXI.
[7] Quaracchi ed. 8: 161.
[8] Raffael e Pazzelli, T.O.R., *Il Terz'Ordine Regolare di S. Francesco attraverso I secoli* (Rome: Curia Generalizia dell'Ordine, 1958), argues, 62-71, that tertiaries living in community were pronouncing religious vows from no later than the 1280s; the evidence is scattered, however, and does not apply to most groups. Cf. Marion A. Habig, O.F.M., and Mark Hegener, O.F.M., *A Short History of the Third Order* (Chicago: Franciscan Herald Press, 1963), 93.

6:14) even suggests an element of primitivism in the author's attitude to the Franciscan heritage. In a passing phrase he requires that the rector *elucidare dubia* ("clarify doubtful matters"), but he seems indifferent to study as such. He praises compassionate brotherly love (*pietas,* ch. 3), patience, discretion, and charity, devoting separate chapters to three of these virtues. These same qualities are inculcated by the example of St. Francis and the earliest Friars in the first and fifth chapters of the *Legend of Perugia.* The importance of the leader's willingness to do as he tells his brethren to do is reinforced by the example of Christ, "Jesus began to do and to teach," (ch. 1:1). The method is drier but the underlying argument is the same as in *Fioretti* (ch. 13), where Francis's devotion to poverty and to preaching is the basic subject, but his imitation of Christ is presented as notable in this, that he expected his followers to preach and to live in poverty only when he had done so himself.

For whom, then, is the treatise intended? Nowhere does the author treat monastic offices other that of the superior; indeed, he never names a specific office and barely alludes to role differentiations of any kind. His comments on caring for beginners, in the first chapter, would be equally appropriate to laymen entering upon a more devout life (the term "novice" does not appear), e.g. by joining a confraternity of the Third Order. In fact, with its advice about exercising newcomers in basic virtues, it would be particularly suitable to those newly converted from lives of wrongdoing. The warning about the very high levels of virtue and wisdom needed in those who have no personal director would apply, of course, with special strength to Beghards, hermits, and other less well disciplined devout persons, of just the kinds among whom few were ordained; where Franciscan ideals and the example of St. Francis were honored but where little or no directly pastoral work was done. It seems clear, therefore, that *De sex alis seraphim* was directed toward the Third Order of St. Francis, specifically the regular communities, since the work treats only of a full religious life, and especially, perhaps, toward Beghard communities that had adopted the Third Order Rule without wholly giving up practices derived from their former status. The work as it stands would be appropriate to this milieu and could well have derived from it.

It is laboring the obvious to note that fourteenth-century piety is often characterized by devotion to St. Francis, a disposition toward mystico-moral interpretation of Scripture, and a concern for the right ordering of the religious life and generally for all forms of dedicated Christian living. Such an attitude was typical of many Beghard and Beguine circle from which a variety of lay conventual bodies took their rise.[9] It was a period of considerable Franciscan literary activity and manuscript production; the *Speculum perfectionis* in its present form[10] and the *Fioretti*[11] date to this period. Rosalind Brooke, in her introduction to the *Legend of Perugia*, lists and describes five different collections that contain, in whole or in part, the Latin text of material attributed to the famous "three companions," along with, in most cases, several other items of Franciscan interest. One of these, the Perugia manuscript itself, contains texts of the rules of all three Orders, while another, from the collection of Collegio San Isidoro, includes an anonymous letter to a nun on the religious life.[12] Thus our document belongs to a time and to circumstances when writings of Franciscan inspiration, including writings concerned with religious life and writings not primarily intended for the Friars, were fairly numerous. On the assumption that *De sex alis seraphim* was

---

[9] Ernst W. McDonnell, *The Beguines and Beghards in Medieval Culture* (New Brunswick: Rutgers University Press, 1954) is the standard treatment in English. There is further specific evidence in an important collection, *Atti del 4° convegno di studi francescani: Prime manifestazioni di vita comunitaria maschile e femminile nel movimento francescano della penitenza* 1215-1447 (Rome: Commissione Storico Internazionale T.O.R. 1982), ed. R. Pazzelli and L. Temperini. On France, Pierre Peano, "Manifestations de la vie en commun parmi les Tertiaires franciscains de la France méridionale," 113-131, especially 114-119; on Belgium, Alfonso Pompei, "Vita comunitaria tra I Penitenti francescani in Belgio," 133-146; on the Netherlands, Servus Gieben, "Vita comunitaria tra I Penitenti francescani nei Paesi Bassi," 147-160. Each of these, and other studies in the same volume, show that there were close, long-standing connections among the Friars Minor, lay penitents such as the Beguines and Beghards, and the Franciscan Third Order. This work is hereafter referred to as *Manifestazioni*.

[10] Theophile Desbonnets, O.F.M., "Introduction," trans. Paul Oligny, O.F.M., to *The Mirror of Perfection* in *St. Francis of Assisi: Omnibus of Sources*, ed. Marion Habig, O.F.M. (Chicago: Franciscan Herald Press, 1975), 1109.

[11] Serge Hughes, "Introduction," *The Little Flowers of St. Francis and Other Franciscan Writings* (New York: Mentor Omega Books, 1964), 17-18.

[12] Rosalind B. Brooke, ed. and trans., *Scripta Leonis, Rufini et Angeli Sociorum S. Francisci: The Writings of Leo, Rufino and Angelo, Companions of St. Francis* (Oxford: Clarendon Press, 1970), 26-37.

Introduction

intended for a tertiary community, or for several such, this text and the social history of the Franciscan Third Order may be expected to throw some light on one another; and incidentally this assumption also makes it easier to understand the value of the work to religious superiors in later, very different circumstances.

From the beginning of the Franciscan movement the Third Order recruited people of widely varied character and way of life, but it appealed chiefly to the middle class and to skilled workers of the towns, to the tradespeople and craft workers, such as cobblers, barbers, smiths, weavers, bakers, and scribes, and to the women of their families. Tertiary communities started with groups of men and women, almost always of the lower and lower middle classes, who already belonged to the Third Order and who decided to forgo marriage and undertake a common life. The transition from the Secular to the Regular Third Order occurred independently in many different places, including Dalmatia, northern and southern France, upper and lower Germany, Holland, Lombardy, Sicily, and Spain.[13] Similar communities with no Franciscan link existed, of course, in great numbers. Among men, these groups usually began as workingmen's associations, or confraternities whose members were all of one trade; weavers were especially prominent in the movement.

The inhabitants of these houses did not observe enclosure and generally supported themselves, at least in the beginning, by continuing their regular secular work. Some groups, on the other hand, were made up of hermits, or of those who worked in a hospice, and there is a reference to a clerical community, consisting entirely of priests and students for the priesthood, at Pamiers in 1404.[14] This is well after the probable date of *De sex alis seraphim*. Outside Italy, where the Secular Third Order was well organized and had many members, the tertiary communities became more prominent than the secular branch and attracted many who were ineligible for ordination or uninterested in pastoral work. The Friars Minor, since the middle of the thirteenth century, had been

---

[13] Essays in *Manifestazioni* treat the Third Order in Spain, southern France, and the Low Countries, Strasbourg, Hungary, Liguria, Milan, Venice, The March, Ferrara, Tuscany, Umbria, Spoleto, Rome, and Messina. Cf. Moorman, 220-21, 418.

[14] Moorman, 419; on care of the poor and of pilgrims and other wayfarers, see Pazzelli, 86-92. On communities of weavers, see *Manifestazioni*, 143.

overwhelmingly an educated and priestly group. Almost all new members were expected to qualify for orders, and even most lay brothers were, in theory, to be educated men. These decisions had probably been reached and acted on as early as 1242 under Haymo of Faversham and were certainly fully in force under the Constitutions of Narbonne, promulgated in 1260. After this, candidates from the laboring classes must have been almost excluded from the Friars, and admission of older men and those with little knowledge of Latin would have been difficult.[15] In fact an actual decision to discourage the recruitment of lay brothers was reached by Haymo of Faversham and maintained by Blessed John of Parma and by St. Bonaventure. It is not unreasonable to suppose that these decisions helped to precipitate the establishment of many conventual bodies within the Third Order. In any case, evidence of such communities begins to appear not many years afterward.

Once established in any town, the tertiary communities often grew, even against opposition, and took deep root. The guardians and lectors of the Friars Minor had many contacts with the Third Order, especially after 1289 when Pope Nicholas IV approved their Rule and confided their direction to the First Order *in Supra montem*.[16] The decree *Santa Romana* of 1317 forbade members of the Third Order to undertake the common life, but so many had already done so, and the movement continued to grow so fast, that a later decree, *Personas vacantes* of 1413, specifically encouraged it.[17] The condemnation of the common life for tertiaries in *Sancta*

---

[15]Laurence C. Landini, O.F.M., *The Causes of the Clericalization of the Order of Friars Minor, 1209-1260, in the Light of the Early Franciscan Sources* (Chicago: For the Pontifical Gregorian University Faculty of Ecclesiastical History, 1968), 129-33; see also Rosalind B. Brooke, *Early Franciscan Government, Elias to Bonaventure* (Cambridge: Cambridge University Press, 1959), 243-245, 273-274, and Giovanni Odoardi, "L'Evoluzione istituzionale dell'ordine codificata da san Bonaventura," in Pompei 163-64.

[16]The Friars Minor, through a custos or by chapter decision, could stipulate the rule to be followed by a community; cf. Clément Schmitt, "Groupements du T.O.R. dans la province de Strasbourg aux XIII-XIVe s.," *Manifestazioni* 178. In the same volume, speaking of Treviso, Paolo Marangon comments that the tertiaries and the Friars had achieved a symbiotic relationship, p. 270 in "Struture di aggregazione dei Penitenti nella Marca Trevigiana nei sec. XIII e XIV." The remark may have a wider application. See also Fidentius Van den Borne, O.F.M., "Analecta de Tertio Ordine," *Archivum Franciscanum Historicum* 9 (1916): 127-33.

[17]Moorman 562; Giovanni Odoardi, "I penitenti francescani nelle bolle pontifici," *Manifestazioni* 26.

Romana seems to be couched in quite general terms, but apparently it did not apply and was never meant to apply to all such communities. Disciples of Peter John Olivi, who was regarded as a heretic, had formed a lay Franciscan community after his death. This, and groups of Joachite tertiaries known as *beguini*, or *fratres de paupere*, which had lapsed into perfectionist and other heresies, fell within the scope of the condemnation. It seems certain that the decree was intended to affect only those whose mystical or reforming propensities were giving the Church serious trouble.[18] The decree eventually interfered with many other tertiary groups,[19] but evidently the movement as a whole, in so far as it was orthodox, received no substantial or lasting check from it.

In the last decades of the thirteenth century and throughout the fourteenth century, the conventual movement spread (there were communities at Monte Casale, Piacenza, Toulouse, and elsewhere before the papal approval of the Third Order Rule in 1289).[20] There were houses with a contemplative orientation, even adopting enclosure for women, especially in Germany beyond the Rhine area,[21] and later to some extent in Italy, where by 1435 the one cloistered Third Order convent, established in 1397 by Angelina of Marsciano had grown to fifteen.[22] Other communities were devotional and, as the term *Penitenti* indicated, penitential. During this period the Friars Minor readily advised women of the artisan classes to become Beguines where a beguinage existed.

---

[18] Raoul Manselli, *Spirituali e Beghini in Provenza* (Roma: Istituto storico Italiano, 1959), 39-40, 144-45.

[19] Pazzelli, 97; Moorman, 422. Evidence from the Inquisitions of Carcassonne and Toulouse (the latter under Bernard Gui) shows how the 1317 decree was used to eliminate the entire Third Order in this part of Provence; cf. Pierre Peano, O.F.M., "Les Béguines du Languedoc ou la crise du T.O.F. dans la France méridionale (XIII-XIV siècles)," *Collectanea Francescana* 47 (1977): 97-117. Similarly Claude Schmitt found that the Third Order Regular groups in the Rhineland barely obtained and retained the church's approval, which was constantly being taken from Beghards and like groups; cf. *Mort d'une hérésie: L'Eglise et les clercs face aux béguines et aux beghards du Rhin supérieur du XIV au XV siècle* (Paris: Mouton, 1978).

[20] Habig and Hegener, 93; Schmitt, *Manifestazioni*, 163-66, lists many towns and cities in the province of Strasbourg where, during the 13th and 14th centuries, tertiary communities were established, usually made up of Beguines and sometimes Beghards.

[21] Brigitte Degler-Spengler, "Der Franziskanische Dritte Orden als Forschungsaufgabe," *Collectanea Francescana* 49 (1979): 95-98.

[22] Moorman, 420; for some problems in interpreting Blessed Angelina's achievement see Anna Filannino, "La B. Angelina dei Conti di Marsciano e le sue fondazioni," *Manifestazioni*, 451-57.

Technically, many of the Beguines under their influence belonged to the Third Order Secular, but since they lived a non-monastic common life with an abundance of community prayer, some charitable undertakings, and Franciscan spiritual direction, the differences between their homes and tertiary convents need not have been great. The Friars helped to set up or reorganize beguinages in Cologne, Toul, Strasbourg, and elsewhere. For the most part the Franciscan beguinages were better organized, more visibly devout, and more concerned with relieving misery and destitution than other houses.[23]

Dayton Phillips sees in the fact that the women in the beguinages could and did move rather freely from one house to another evidence that the community life had economic purposes primarily rather than religious motives. He observes that this was an affordable way for respectable single women with limited earning powers, many of whom came into the towns from the surrounding countryside and almost none of whom were from wealthy families, to sustain themselves decently. Economic motivations need not be denied, but what the evidence really shows is that life in one Beguine household was similar enough to the life in another, especially if all were under Franciscan direction, that an individual could find her place in almost any of them.[24] Transfers from one house to another were, in all probability, often made, in houses of men as well as in those of women, for the sake of a better psychological fit in the community, or to provide more help to the frail and sick. A truly economic motive for such moves was no doubt often present, e.g. arranging for an untrained sister or brother to live with a more skillful member of the community and to become his or her apprentice.

Beghard communities also became Franciscan, and here a more fully monastic life seems to have been adopted than in non-contemplative women's houses. By 1346 at least seventeen Belgian Beghard houses had become regularized, and from then on and

---

[23]Dayton Phillips, *Beguines in Medieval Strasbourg* (Ann Arbor: Edwards Brothers, 1941), 116-26, 170, 177-78.
[24]Phillips, 126, 156-59, 173; cf. McDonnell, 276. By 1443 each house in the Liège diocese had a priest superior; the motherhouse of the group was at Zepperen and in general there is an air of the fully formed congregation about it (Moorman, 563; Pompei, *Manifestazioni*, 140-41).

throughout the fifteenth century other Beghard communities tended to follow suit.[25] Often such houses continued, even after adopting the Franciscan Rule, to recruit members only from a single trade. The members included few if any priests and largely supported themselves by continuing the trades which they had learned and practiced as laymen. Their commitment was to community life, rather than, initially, to community property or to a strict vow of poverty, although their day-to-day living standard was probably austere. The slow change of Beghard groups into regular tertiary bodies may be appreciated by considering some dates. A Beghard house at Léau had made the change as early as 1291; a house of Beghard weavers at Aerschot, which had existed since 1283, did so in 1325; those of Bois-le-Duc and Maestricht had become tertiaries in the mid-fourteenth century, while Ophem's beghards did not become Franciscan until 1474. All of these houses were made up of laymen, manual workers who led a conventual life and took on various charitable works.[26]

What of the life of the communities for which *De sex alis seraphim* was composed? They lived under a number of different and mutually inconsistent rules and yet could speak of St. Francis as "our Father." Their superiors required no advice about studies, or apostolic and charitable works, but needed to be reminded of the importance of care for the sick brethren and of patience with the spiritually weak, a patience which must not itself become weakness in the face of incorrigibility or of rebellion. The communities had some priests, but apparently not many. Vocations were numerous but not always fervent. In the second chapter, when discussing the four kinds of good religious, the author seems to have in mind persons whose commitment to the religious life may have arisen from convenience almost as much as from fervor; his first category consists of those who are sociable and peaceful, not notable for misbehavior, but not especially holy. Poverty, one of the traditional vows of religion and especially dear to Franciscans,

---

[25] McConnell, 257-65.
[26] McDonnell, 255; Pompei, *Manifestazioni*, 140, mentions groups at Brussels, Ghent, St. Trond, Malines, and elsewhere as transferring from the Beghard to the Franciscan tertiary status, or as adding the latter to the former, and other authors in that volume refer to many other instances.

is mentioned along with patience, humility, and sobriety (ch. 6:6), suggesting a more fluid situation than that of an order with vows.

The community possessed a church to which lay people could come to attend Mass and at least part of the Divine Office; it is unclear whether the brothers celebrated the whole Office, and also whether any of the priests were authorized to hear confessions. The community needed the work of every member to keep going, and relied as well, perhaps imprudently, on the alms of the faithful. There is no hint that the religious could be moved from one house to another, nor did they observe enclosure. If there was any organized commitment to external activities (and there may have been none), it probably involved only a minority of the brethren. Conceivably it included preaching, but may equally well have been confined to works of charity. If, in fact, any preaching was carried out, there seems to have been no reason to fear that it would be doctrinally unorthodox or insubordinate to the Church. In the author's judgment the brothers were more likely to endanger than to improve themselves by outside activities, and their superiors ran particularly serious risks of excessive involvement in administrative duties and in the piling up of property (ch. 6:13). The communities were to some degree in competition with forms of ascetic life which involved no well-defined headship (ch. 1). These characteristics are far more consistent with what is known of the regular tertiary communities than of the Friars Minor or of any other religious of the period.

Generally, where the Beghard movement was not active, there is some evidence of continuity between earlier, non-Franciscan penitent movements and the formation of regular tertiary communities. The link is one of spiritual orientation rather than of institutional or organizational forms. Not uncommonly, as at Viterbo, one of the chief starting points for the community movement among tertiaries, there were various contacts with groups of lay penitents on the part of Third Order hermits, extending from the thirteenth to the fifteenth centuries; there were local personalities, especially St. Rose of Viterbo, with considerable influence; and there were several different bodies of tertiaries living in community, founded at different times and under different circumstances. In Viterbo's case, efforts to bring about unity among these groups, despite determined support on the part of Pope Nicholas V in 1447, were only successful under Pope Paul II in 1467, well over a hundred years after the first communities were founded in the region.[27]

Assuredly, one strong source of appeal in the communities of regular tertiaries was that Beghards and Beguines, who were in danger from the Inquisition after the Vienne decretal of 1311, had some protection from it if they had Franciscan affiliation, since the decree *Etsi Apostolicae* of 1319 forbade the application of the Vienne condemnation of beguinages to houses of the Third Order.[28]

It is clear, however, that by no means all Third Order communities had Beghard or Beguine backgrounds. Whatever fears of tertiary heterodoxy the hierarchy entertained, moreover, and however justified they may sometimes have been, it would be a mistake to suppose that Franciscan affiliation was a frequent mode of concealment for actual heresy. It is more probable that participants in devotional confraternities, service-oriented religious societies, and Beghard and Beguine groups enrolled as Franciscan precisely in order to separate themselves more effectively from heretical tendencies. Thus in Vicenza the lay penitential groups were suspect of heresy, and there is no evidence of institutional derivation from them, nor of close personal ties between their members and the founders of the local Franciscan Third Order, whether the latter remained laymen or eventually formed religious communities.[29]

Third Order affiliation was attractive not only to those already part of devotional movements, but to laypeople without previous organizational ties. The Spanish communities in León seem to have originated from previously unaffiliated faithful.[30]

---

[27]Vincenzo Pettriccione, T.O.R., "Como nacque la provincia Romana del T.O.R. francescana: Viterbo: S. Maria della Ginestra," *Analecta T.O.R.* 12 (1972): 561-93.

[28]Pazzelli, 97-98; McDonnell, 526-30. Extreme zeal in enforcing the decrees against the Fraticelli and other suspect groups made trouble for some entirely orthodox Beghards, but for some time, according to Pazzelli, the Third Order communities were safe from them, as the Pope had intended; see his article, "Giovanni XXII e la *Altissimi in Divinis*," *Manifestazioni*, 53-56.

[29]Giovanni Mantese, "'Fratres et sorores de poenitencia' di S. Francesco in Vicenza dal XIII al XV secolo," in *Miscellanea Gilles Gerard Meerssemann* (Padua: Antenore, 1970), 695-714.

[30]Odlio G.-Parente, "Provincia de Terciarios regulares franciscanos de Leon," *Archivo Ibero-americano* 36 (1976), No. 144: 495-508. This essay on the Spanish tertiary

The enthusiasm which brought a group into existence did not always last: in Spoleto a member of the Third Order had founded a hospital in 1295, and for some time tertiaries maintained it. By 1398 *fratres antiqui non existunt* ("the old community has died out") but the hospital itself continued. In 1436 the Foligno tertiaries, both brothers and sisters, decided to get it back under Third Order control, and did so in 1448, only to lose it to the Benedictines in 1451.[31] It is clear that there were wide variations in the form of life of different houses, in the time, manner, and degree of reformist influence on their establishment, in their capacity to survive, their attachment to the Friars Minor, their resistance to heterodoxy, and their relations with the hierarchy. Modern historical generalizations about the Third Order, in that they are confused, mutually inconsistent, and not fully applicable to many specific communities, mirror historical reality more effectively than a more orderly presentation can do.

Late medieval Ireland provides a fairly well-documented example of the establishment of tertiary community life in the complete absence of prior lay renewal movements. Growth of Third Order community life, after its introduction in or shortly before the 1420s, was rapid and extensive. The five fourteenth-century references to what may be tertiary communities in Ireland are all questionable, but by 1426 members were numerous and houses had begun to multiply. They had churches, at Killeenbrennan in the diocese of Tuam, County Mayo, as early as 1428, and not long after in other places. Several members were priests, and occasionally canons and vicars resigned their benefices to join them. Before 1450 they had monasteries in Ulster and in five Gaelic-speaking places in the west. There were forty-seven houses (not necessarily all contemporary with one another) during the fifteenth century, of

---

communities of the fourteenth through the sixteenth centuries points out that they had no direct ties to the Franciscan Observance (i.e. the First Order) until 1568, under St. Pius V.

[31] Mario Sensi, "Vicende del T.O.R. nella Valle spoletana," *Analecta T.O.R.* 129 (1978): 49-88. Pazzelli, 104-106, discusses the loss of a popular Marian shrine, suffered by the Third Order because the local bishop no longer trusted the quality of its members. Similarly, Martino Bertagna, "Origine e sviluppo del Terz'Ordine Regolare in Toscana" (*Manifestazioni*, 377-78), narrates the shifts in control of a hospice at Montepulciano, directed by a male Third Order community for many years in the 15th century, then controlled by the city itself for some time, and eventually turned over to tertiary Sisters in 1513.

which about forty survived well into Reformation times, located in eighteen dioceses and fifteen counties; community life did not entirely disappear until after 1616. The ruins of Killenbrennan, the principal house, are extensive. It may have served as a double monastery for a while, but after the mid-fifteenth century references to tertiary sisters disappear. By 1456 Father Thomas Uruayn, T.O.R., a canon lawyer, was appointed visitor for all the Irish houses. Yet it seems that Killeenbrennan, where he resided, did not function like a motherhouse in a modern congregation, since foundations could be made independently of it; e.g. the community at Rosskirk, County Mayo, made a foundation at Straidkelly, County Antrim. The brothers served parishes and conducted schools for boys.[32] The stubborn strength of these communities, surviving under persecution for nearly a century, indicates the popular and widespread character of the impetus from which they arose.

The efforts of the hierarchy and the papacy to manage the tertiary movement were only intermittently, and never completely, successful. In a sense the Third Order Regular attained a "definitive status" after Nicholas V's decree *Pastoralis officii* in 1447.[33] But old groups continued to disintegrate, new ones to be formed, and Franciscan affiliation to cover a multitude of types of conventual existence. Sometimes, as in Utrecht, tertiaries who lived a common life took no vow of poverty (thus, those in the community who were clergy could receive benefices).[34] On the whole it seems fair to say that the movement for which *De sex alis seraphim* was composed remained essentially just that, a movement of fervent laity and of some priests, responding in a great variety of ways to a religious call in which Franciscan inspiration was only one element.

Let us try to describe the most typical form which this conventual movement took. As with other lay religious houses,

---

[32] *Materials for the History of the Franciscan Province of Ireland A.D. 1230-1450*, ed. E. B. Fitzmaurice, O.F.M., and A. G. Little (Manchester University Press, 1920; British Society of Franciscan Studies, 9), map. p. ii; Introduction by A. G. Little, pp. xxxi-xxxii; pp. 194-95, 197-98, 198n., 202. Aubrey Gwynn and R. Neville Hadcock, *Medieval Religious Houses: Ireland* (London: Longman, 1970), 263-68.

[33] Louis Secondo, T.O.R., "The Mission of the Third Order Regular of St. Francis in the Modern World," *Analecta T.O.R.* 130 (1978): 139-56.

[34] Frédégand d'Anvers, O.F.M. Cap., "Le Tiers-Ordre de St. François d'Assise," *Etudes Franciscaines* 34 (1922): 199-201.

there were cases in which a tertiary community was set up, from its inception, with a charitable work in mind, e.g. the care of orphans. We have seen that some communities, especially of women, were contemplative. What seems to have been much more common, however, is a development along these lines:

1. A group of devout people, men or women, already acquainted with one another through sharing a trade and perhaps guild membership decide to live in common and to make a commitment to religious celibacy. Franciscan influence, and admission to the Third Order, might precede this initial decision, coincide with it, or follow it—even, sometimes, in the second or third generation of the community. But one way or another many such houses adopted the Third Order Rule. Franciscan attachment does not impede the retention of devout customs, or even of rules, derived from other sources. When the community is first formed, and for long thereafter, all or most of the members continue to work at their trade.

2. Recruitment to the house is chiefly or entirely among other people engaged in the same trade. There is a regular round of common prayers, a head, sometimes known as the minister,[35] or the superior,[36] and often close ties with the Friars Minor because of similar spiritual ideals as well as through reception of counsel and instruction from officials of the First Order.[37] Some members begin to work full time within the community residence, either at their regular trade, especially if it is weaving, or on community business. They obtain their own chapel, to which lay people sometimes come for prayers.

---

[35] The Zepperen brothers used this term, another indication of their close approximation to a traditional order, in their statutes of 1487 (J. Daris, *Notices sur les églises du diocèse de Liège* 13 [1887], 104; quoted in McDonnell, 144).

[36] McDonnell, 256; the Bruges Beghards may have used this term.

[37] Moorman, 421, 565; H. Roggen, "Les relations du Premier Ordre franciscain avec le Tiers-Ordre au xiiie siècle," *Collectanea Francescana* 43 (1973): 199-209. Pazzelli, 94-95, acknowledges that the Friars were not consistently zealous in offering pastoral care to tertiary communities. St. Bonaventure himself feared that the Friars would do themselves more harm than good unless they kept their distance; cf. Gabriele Andreozzi, T.O.R., "San Bonaventura e l'*Ordo Poenitentiae*," Pompei, 359-62. But many of the articles in *Manifestazioni*, and much other evidence, show that the papal desire for tertiary communities to come under the supervision of the Friars met with significant cooperation, and *De sex alis seraphim* itself, as interpreted here, is a further instance.

3. In a few years, a definite service has been undertaken by the community. Perhaps it often happened that an elderly weaver, cobbler, etc., left without family and unable to work, was taken in by the tertiary community belonging to his own trade and cared for while he lived. It is of some significance that Leo X's Rule of 1521, which in other respects is so different from that of 1289, takes up assistance to the sick from it. In all likelihood, even communities that had no programmatic service had some degree of commitment to care of the sick, e.g. sick members of the craft guild to which the brothers belonged. Eventually the brothers become known for their care of the sick and adopt this work as a basic element in their lives.

Perhaps the laymen in the guild, knowing that their religious colleagues include a few who are literate at least in the vernacular and have had time for study, ask that their sons be given some rudimentary schooling. Elsewhere a new recruit to the community feels called to undertake some service, such as running a hospice for pilgrims, and persuades the house to sponsor and assist him in it. On their own or through the suggestion of others, many communities undertook some charitable work. Moorman mentions guest houses, schools, hospitals, and visitation of the sick in their homes. Eventually they found that they needed many members to devote themselves fulltime to work within the house, and for the ordination of some to the priesthood. Many communities gave up their previous close ties to a specific guild.[38] Thus they became more like modern religious congregations; but for many years there would continue to be a body of community members who had joined it only with a view to their own spiritual security.

This, in all likelihood, is the monastic situation for which *De sex alis seraphim* was written. Intended initially, perhaps, for a group that had gone no further than the second stage, its advice was suited both in manner and in tone to the circumstances of the third stage too. Only once does the author speak of the ordinary faithful, *simplices fideles,* as the direct object of the work of the monastery and then (ch. 7:8) it is in connection with *clericos celebrare divina,* ("clergy conducting divine services") in the church, and without implying that many members will be clergy.

---

[38]Moorman, 568.

Earlier, observing that it is edifying to celebrate the Liturgy properly, in a context suggesting that he has in mind the edification of the monastery itself, he notes that laymen as well as clergy have their proper roles to play therein (ch. 2:7). It is an observation that would have been unlikely to occur to someone writing for the Friars Minor themselves. His warning against excessively early ordination and against giving young priests too much responsibility (ch. 4:3) would represent an impractical ideal for the Friars, an Order with large and growing responsibilities for preaching, hearing confessions, and missionary work. The treatise implies that when candidates are accepted into the community their suitability for religious life is to be tested, and only later, as part of a separate process, is any decision to be made concerning holy orders. It is also assumed that the community will encourage men to prepare for the priesthood chiefly for service within the monastery itself. The Friars Minor, well before the fourteenth century, indeed before St. Bonaventure became Minister General, had taken opposite decisions on these points.[39] In discussing spiritual weakness in the brethren, the first remedy the author of the treatise proposes is to "prevent them from going out on their own away from the community" (ch. 3:8), advice compatible with the Regular tertiary way of life but scarcely applicable to the Friars.

Where the writer seems ready to turn to the subject of pastoral work (in a catalogue of things that go wrong and require the rector's patience) he is typically vague: "[The brothers] give up tasks that would strengthen other Christians to gain for themselves opportunities to beg" (*aedificationes animarum pro questu vendere*, ch. 4:3). *Aedificatio* (literally, "upbuilding") is a term with a broad meaning and need not imply either pastoral or charitable activity outside the community. He several times insists on the importance of everyone in the community working (e.g. ch. 5:2), and uses the term *labor*, which certainly can apply to ordinary manual

---

[39]The warning against promoting men too easily to the priesthood, however, does have a parallel in legislation for the Friars Minor that was prepared by St. Bonaventure himself. The Constitutions of Narbonne (ch. 6, 15-16) advise that the choice of men to be ordained priests or to be made confessors should be made as carefully as appointments to study at the universities. The advice does not seem to have been widely followed.

work. He urgently warns against too much involvement in secular business and the piling up of property (ch. 6:11,14). Warnings against excessive involvement in the worldly affairs of commerce are, of course, traditional in the advice given to monastic heads; the earliest examples go back to the writings on the task of the *abba* in the *sketes* of the Egyptian desert. Still, such comments are especially pointed if directed to tertiary Beghards who were sometimes in trouble with civic officials concerning their business deals.[40]

The overall picture, then, is of a member of the Friars Minor writing at a time of expansion of the Regular tertiary movement and aware that many of the new recruits to this form of the religious life, however sincere their piety, would be better able to live a sociable, honest, and peaceful life (ch. 2:2) and perhaps to take part in certain works of charity, than to undertake a pastoral mission. Even in treating of the deeply devout brethren, he mentions only the virtues that edify the community itself, and he recommends those with a desire to lead others to God (not a large percentage of the community as he envisions it) as potential heads within the monastery itself, seemingly without expecting them to find an outlet for their zeal among laymen. When he does speak of edifying one's neighbor (ch. 2:9), it is only by good example. All of this makes good sense if he is writing for Regular tertiary bodies, not all of which have an external ministry, none of which is primarily devoted to pastoral activities, and most of whose members are spiritually and in socioeconomic status closely akin to the men among whom the Beghard movement found most of its recruits.

Like Salimbene in the thirteenth century, the author of the treatise displays a gentlemanly or bourgeois distaste for singularity, a deep respect for monastic tradition, community life, and good order, and a disposition to interpret Franciscan ideals somewhat in terms of St. Bernard's teaching on the religious life. His teaching seems, indeed, almost calculated to protect the communities for whose rectors he is writing from the charges

---

[40] Adalbert de Vogüé, O.S.B., *Community and Abbot in the Rule of St. Benedict*, 1 (Kalamazoo: Cistercian Publications, 1979): 81; Moorman, 149-50 McDonnell, 363-65.

leveled by Salimbene against the *apostolici* of his own day. This can hardly be literally the case, since Salimbene's work was probably unknown at the time. But the similarity of spirit is observable in Salimbene's accusations against the *apostolici*, a group of lay practitioners of the *vita apostolica* which Gerard Segarello founded after he was refused entrance into the Friars Minor.[41] Salimbene condemns them "for not having a properly constituted superior, for going about the countryside singly without a companion, for wandering about without reason or utility, for not observing discipline, for not providing instruction and formation for their novices, for constantly moving from one house to another, for wanting to preach and to teach without having theological training and ecclesiastical approval, and for begging alms without working."[42] The author of *De sex alis seraphim*, a half-century or more later and independently of Salimbene, warmly recommends submission to a rector, which is opposed to the first of these charges, and mentions the problem related to the seventh: early and ill-prepared assignment to preaching and hearing confessions.

Only two items on the list in Salimbene do not reappear, and if the communities for which the author wrote were independent of one another these were irrelevant. There are few respects in which the author was original and, probably, none in which he was controversial. The influence of St. Bernard appears in the very first sentence of the Prologue: "Give instruction to a wise man and he grows wiser still" (Prv. 9:9). This quotation appears in St. Bernard's *Sermones in Cantica* 23 (3:5), largely devoted to the duties of a religious superior. This chapter of Proverbs was a favorite topic of meditations on the Church during the patristic period and its ninth verse appears in some of the earliest monastic texts, those associated with St. Anthony the Hermit, at the end of his second, third, and seventh letters.[43]

---

[41]David. L. Jeffrey. *The Early English Lyric and Franciscan Spirituality*, (Lincoln: University of Nebraska Press, 1975), 64.

[42]Duane V. Lapsanski, *Evangelical Perfection: An Historical Examination of the Concept in the Early Franciscan Sources* (St. Bonaventure, N.Y.: Franciscan Institute, 1977), 211-12, 215-16, summarizing material from pp. 393-414 of Giusèppe Scalia's edition of *Cronica* by Salimbene de Adam (Bari: Laterza, 1966).

[43]*The Letters of St. Anthony the Great*, ed. Derwas J. Chitty (Oxford: SLG Press, 1975), 8, 11, 28; cf. also *The Letters of Ammonas*, trans. Derwas J. Chitty (Fairacres, Oxford: SLG Press, 1979), 2.

The author shows no concern about heresy, even in his sharpest, most aggrieved laments about the scandal given by bad religious. His sole reference to the pope and the bishops (ch. 1:3) is non-polemical. He gives no advice specifically about novices, although much of what he says has to do with the direction of the spiritually immature and is relevant to beginners. He points out that there are many, *rudes in religione, qui interna non sapiunt* ("unperceptive religious who have no taste for the interior life" ch. 4:3); such persons might well include educated men but the remark applies with special force to the problems of a superior of a community most of whose members had little schooling. His complaints about failures and abuses never hint at a weakening movement; rather, he vocally regrets the large number of religious (ch. 4:3). The mood of the work as a whole differs little from what one finds in exhortations written in the twentieth century before the Second Vatican Council. Such recent works, despite the weakness of the argument from silence, constitute evidence that such Church problems as the Modernist crisis had little or no impact on many religious congregations. In the same way, *De sex alis seraphim*, in its blandness and communitarian introversion, suggests that there was a sizable body of Regular tertiary houses which lived placidly without controversy and worked (more or less) steadily without prominence.

In late medieval society, workers and trades people—among the latter especially those who had arrived at no prominence and only a little prosperity—were somewhat readily recruited into religious movements that tended toward the unorthodox and the extravagant. The Franciscans, of all fully constituted orders, themselves most nearly retained the character of a movement, and the Friars probably had more contacts with the praise-singers, flagellants, penitents, and the confraternities of all kinds, than did most other clergy. If their fervor was doctrinally above reproach and they had few moral scandals to live down, the Franciscans were welcome to give such groups direction in their devotions and works of charity, in some cases forming them into another fraternity of the Third Order.

If their public conduct was likely to astonish ordinary, less devout people, this was not necessarily a bad thing. A bishop might interpret astonishment as a kind of edification when it attended the shouting, singing, scourging demonstrations of a group, sometimes of tertiaries, whose loyalty to the Catholic Church was clear and who were to that extent a kind of inoculation of the total population against the infection of heresy. At the same time, the troublesome element of extreme enthusiasm, always ready to get out of hand whether by accusing the bishop himself of poor leadership, finding a false doctrine to propound, or carrying odd devotional practices too far, would always be of concern to the authorities. A Friar Minor, especially one with some sympathy for the concerns of the bishops and some experience as a superior, would be more likely to want to encourage groups such as those for which this treatise was written, which, whether or not they originated in a wave of enthusiasm, had settled into a more commonplace style and level of devotion.

Lucid and fervent rather than eloquent or profound, *De sex alis seraphim* commends the virtues of discretion, brotherly love, zeal, good example, patience, and devotion. The treatise is designed to assist communities whose function was, simply and almost wholly, to live the religious life. Lay religious in active orders today have a life like this, and it is of some importance to recognize that, theologically, they suffer no diminution in their intrinsic character thereby. For many generations, however, entire congregations of this kind have not been seen. Clearly, this mode of life is hard to sustain for a whole religious house of any size, however well suited to individual religious. In the fourteenth century also, such communities suffered from a paradoxical instability. When they abandoned crafts for the *opera charitatis* ("works of charity"), they increased their value to society and probably appealed to a more zealous type of recruit, but they made their economic condition highly precarious. A religious house of men could secure more gifts and bequests if it contained priests. The lay character of the community, one reason for its existence in the first place, is thus compromised.[44] The unspecialized nature of religious life as

---

[44]In an unpublished paper, "The *opera charitatis* and Twelfth Century Spirituality," James Broadman of the University of Central Arkansas has shown that,

originally lived, a search for salvation leading to community life and asceticism under a leader whose only pastoral concern was the community itself, had remained a reality, though a diminished one, in the complexities of the later Middle Ages.[45] The changes undergone by the vowed tertiaries represent another step in the gradual decline of this ancient tradition.

The fourteenth century with its many crises was not only a time of growth in religious fervor and of expansion of the Regular tertiary movement, but of other signs of the popularity of the Franciscan spirit. This, perhaps, explains the way in which *De sex alis seraphim* came to be attributed to the well-known and deeply admired theologian, St. Bonaventure, whose works were widely read and extracted. There is the best possible literary evidence, Dante's, that in the fourteenth century St. Bonaventure was admired for teaching that religious superiors should put pastoral duties above their administrative responsibilities. In *Paradiso* the pilgrim meets Bonaventure among the savants in the circle of the sun:

> Io son la vita di Bonaventura
> da Bagnoregio, che nei grandi offici,
> sempre posposi la sinistra cura.

> I am the life of Bonaventure of Bagnoregio,
> who in high offices always put away
> the cares of the left hand.
> Canto XII, ll. 127-130.

"La sinistra cura," clearly refers to material concerns. There were many pseudo-Bonaventurian works in circulation, not least the immensely influential *Meditationes vitae Christi*.[46] David of Augsburg (d. 1272) wrote several works applying Bonaventure's general spiritual teaching to monastic life.[47] A Catalan Franciscan, Francesc Eiximenis, wrote a life of Christ, which was translated into the vernacular with the addition of large extracts from St.

---

at least in Spain prior to the foundation of the Franciscans, works of service were often both a destabilizing factor and a reason for being of lay religious communities.

[45] Jean Leclercq, O.S.B., *Contemplative Life* (Kalamazoo: Cistercian Publications, 1978), 6.

[46] John V. Fleming, *An Introduction to the Franciscan Literature of the Middle Ages*. (Chicago: Franciscan Herald Press, 1977), 212.

[47] Fleming, 216-25.

Bonaventure's writings.[48] *De sex alis seraphim*, because of its somewhat misleading title, was readily confused with the *Itinerarium*.[49] There exists another Franciscan work of this era, *De septem itineribus aeternitatis*, on the seven steps to union with God, which uses scriptural allegory to structure a spiritual teaching in a somewhat similar way.[50] We need not suppose, therefore, that deliberate fraud entered into the mistaken attribution of *De sex alis seraphim* to Bonaventure. An anonymous work of this type was easy to mistake for one of Bonaventure's own compositions, and the very obscurity of the treatise (only a few manuscripts exist, not all of which are known to be of Franciscan provenance, and most of them are actually later than the first printed edition of 1495),[51] would prevent recognition of the mistake during the short period when attribution might have been questioned.

The conditions that led the author to shape his presentation almost entirely with the inner good of the monastery in mind, in the different circumstances of the Counter-Reformation, made this little work popular with the Jesuits. In their often large houses the rector was usually too preoccupied with direction of the community as such either to undertake external pastoral work himself or directly to oversee the pastoral aspect of the work of his subordinates. The necessity of an internal focus, both spiritual and administrative, in the work of the religious superior of an active community, has persisted to our own day, and has even become a point of asceticism recommended to one whose original motives for entering religious life may be presumed to have been conventionally apostolic. With that necessity has persisted the usefulness of this anonymous fourteenth-century treatise, a document in the tradition of Saints Francis and Bonaventure but not of their times or circumstances; a short, once influential discussion

---

[48] A. G. Haug, "La Vita Christi de Fr. Francesc Eiximenis, O.F.M. (1340?-1409) como tratado de Cristologia para seglares," *Archivum Franciscanum Historicum* 71 (1978): 37-64.

[49] Brady, 106. The earliest seeming reference to the work, by Bartholomew of Pisa, c. 1385-99, is probably really to the *Itinerarium*. The first reference mentioned in the Quaracchi edition, p. LX, and not rejected by Fr. Brady, is by Gulielmus Vorilongus, c. 1450. A date in the mid-fourteenth century is probable in view of the strength of the Third Order movement, including its conventual elements, in this period, but it may be somewhat later.

[50] Fleming, 213.

[51] Brady, 106; Quaracchi edition LXI.

of the character of a Christian leader, in which their spirit is reflected and somewhat distorted through an honest and zealous utterance, intellectually limited but genuinely helpful to and beyond its intended audience.

Philip F. O'Mara

Prologue

"Give instruction to a wise man, and he will be still wiser" (Prov. 9:9). The wise take advantage of their opportunities. They find something to deepen their wisdom in the least important occasion; even another person's dullness will often help them become more perceptive.

This essay has been written for heads of Christian communities who are new to their responsibilities and for those who will soon take on such tasks. It aims to give them a chance to devote more thought to the precise discernment of good and evil. Much of our attention will be given to various errors, but the goal of this discussion is to teach heads to be diligent in calling their communities to more spiritual and service-oriented conduct.

Those who commit themselves to life in a Christian community and accept a call to serve within it as leaders ought to study the many topics treated in this book and more besides. Men and women of real wisdom, after all, have been willing to study the behavior of brute animals in order to find ideas that would apply to their own arts and skills.

Chapter One

The Need for Christian Leaders

1. "I am writing these instructions to you so that . . . you may know how one ought to behave in the household of God, which is the church of the living God" (1Tim. 3:14-15). Paul wrote twice to Timothy, whom he had made bishop of the church at Ephesus, to teach him how to act in exercising the authority committed to him. Timothy had already learned to live a holy life as an individual Christian; now Paul wanted to teach him how to exercise authority over other Christians in a way that would be useful to them and meritorious for him. For while living peacefully among equals and submitting humbly to authority call for certain abilities in a man, providing useful leadership demands others.

Bernard of Clairvaux writes: "Understand this: many men live quietly enough under the personal rule of another, but if you remove that yoke, prove unable to be quiet any longer—unable to keep themselves from any kind of wrongdoing. Furthermore, you find that certain men live, to the best of their ability, in peace with everyone, and hardly need a master at all; yet they are not suited to headship themselves. 'According to the measure of faith which God has assigned' (Rom. 12:3), they are content with a kind of good mediocrity. They know how to live with the members of the community in peace and harmony. But once they are placed over their brethren, their leadership is useless, foolish, and harmful. Those who know how to serve as leaders are better, therefore, than the other two kinds of people."[1]

For this reason Moses was instructed not to put just anyone in charge of the people, but to choose out of the entire people those men who were expert and capable of serving as judges (Exod. 18:21-22). Someone who accepts responsibility for making others good should have already learned the self-discipline necessary for goodness, so that his Christian virtue has become habitual through

---

[1] *Sermons on The Song of Songs*, 23, n. 8.

constant practice. "Jesus began to do and teach" (Acts 1:1): the Lord is presented as first doing the things he later taught.

Why Have Leaders?

2. Beginners in the Christian life need a director so that they can be taught what they do not know: "You need someone to teach you . . . the first principles of God's word" (Heb. 5:12). There is much that they must learn for the sake of their own salvation and spiritual progress—what to avoid; what to take pleasure in; what to do, hope for, fear; how to tell the lesser from the greater evils and the good from the better.

Furthermore, it is not enough only to know what is good. A Christian must also be trained to practice these virtues. Medical students are expected to study their material and then to develop their skills by working with the sick, because practice imprints knowledge on the mind more effectively than study alone. This applies to the skills of every discipline. Yet often those who have not mastered their trade are reluctant to take the trouble to improve their skills. They need at times to have someone who will insist that they practice.

The heads of a Christian community are therefore accustomed to exercise the people in their care in various virtues that they need to acquire, such as humility, brotherly love, patience, obedience, sexual morality, devotion, sobriety, silence, and others. Those committed to the Christian life should be led to practice these virtues and to overcome the vices opposed to them: "Bring them up in the discipline and instruction of the Lord" (Eph. 6:4). The more our virtue advances, the more our vices grow weak.

Beginners in Christian life must also be guided, so that they will not be dragged into sin, or for that matter, into imprudent practices of virtue. The fact is that the spiritually immature, those not yet cleansed from the effects of sin, are often held back from sin more by fear of man than fear of God. It is to their advantage to be under the direction of a guide who can pull them out of danger, like a mother who protects her children from drowning or falling prey to wild animals. "For wisdom will come into your heart, and knowledge will be pleasant to your soul; discretion will watch over you; understanding will guard you; delivering you from the way of evil, from men of perverted speech" (Prov. 2:10-12).

Finally, leaders should devote themselves to correcting beginners in the spiritual life, because the force of sin is still alive in them to drag them down to a lower standard of conduct, just as a fever pushes a sick person into more serious illness, or a neglected wound becomes infected. The more involved one has been in a fault, the harder it is to rub out the stain by one's own power. One needs the help of a stronger person.

That is why God has willed that more mature Christians should have authority over beginners. In this way, if the beginners fall into sin or any neglectful or reckless conduct, the more mature can turn them back to righteousness through their warnings, penalties, corrections, and demands. The less mature, left to their own judgment, may well fail to see anything wrong in their bad conduct. Indifferent to their guilt, they will wallow in it longer and sink more deeply. Therefore they must humbly accept their director's advice, for a sick man cannot be healed unless he obeys the doctor.

Sinful passions are the infirmities characteristic of the human condition. Christ has given the leaders of his people the right to act on behalf of the weaker brethren and to overcome what troubles them: "Convince some, who doubt" (Jude 22). And, "he gave them power and authority over all demons and to cure diseases" (Luke 9:1).

Who Does Not Need a Director?

3. Those who wish to live without a director should be so enlightened by knowledge that they are never mistaken about anything that they need to know. They should be divinely qualified to discern spirits, so that no man or demon or impression of their own can ever deceive them as to what is good: "In any and all circumstances I have learned the secret of facing [my condition]" (Phil. 4:12).

Such persons should also be so filled with devout fervor that they faithfully commit themselves, without urging from anyone else, to the best possible expression of every virtuous practice:

"Forgetting what lies behind and straining forward to what lies ahead, I press on" (Phil. 3:13-14).

Again, they should be so inclined to love what is good that they find horror in everything evil. They must carefully abstain from anything that could give scandal and treat all people inoffensively and peaceably: "Give no offense to Jews or to Greeks" (1Cor. 10:32).

Next, they should be so humble that they are not puffed up by their own goodness, nor presume to lack all evils. In other words, they can judge precisely all their faults of thought, word, and omission, and then amend themselves through strict correction.

Finally, they should be so steady in all these virtues that no trifle or distraction, to say nothing of genuine difficulty or fear, can change their position: "Who shall separate us from the love of Christ?" (Rom. 8:35).

It is difficult to practice such virtues as these, and so there are few suited to life without submission to a head. For the same reason, those who direct others to a better and wiser life must themselves be subject to headship, right on up to the Sovereign Pontiff, who, as vicar of Christ, is the head of the whole Church militant.

4. Those who should exercise leadership need to have different virtues. They need certain virtues in order to conduct their own lives without reproach, others to obey their own guides humbly, and still others to give worthwhile direction to the people in their care, calling them on to better things. A person responsible for teaching others how to practice the virtues ought to possess them all in the highest degree. For practical purposes, however, one can reduce the qualities needed in a guide of souls to six that are especially important. They are like the six wings of the seraphim (Isa. 6:2), the angels who are the vanguard of the heavenly host; these wings are a means of both action and defense.

And so, no doubt, the Lord appeared to our holy Father Francis in the likeness of a Seraph, sealing him, in that glorious vision, with the Stigmata of the Passion, to show that those who govern communities well have need of these spiritual wings. The same idea applies to the four six-winged living creatures in Revelations (4:8).

Chapter Two

Zeal For Righteousness

1. The first characteristic that the director of a community needs is zeal for righteousness, so that his heart is troubled whenever he finds anything unjust in himself or in others. We judge a person's goodness by the extent to which that person feels a pure and growing hatred for evil; for to the extent that we love something, we grieve at its destruction. Consequently we are accustomed to call four kinds of religious people "good."

2. The first are those who do no evil, yet do not devote themselves faithfully to doing good. They live with other people quietly and peaceably, offending no one and giving no scandal: "These men were very good to us and we suffered no harm" (1Sam. 25:15). We usually call such individuals good if their manners are inoffensive and they conduct themselves sociably with everyone, even though they seem to lack other, more positive virtues. In the same way we speak of baptized infants as good.

3. There is a second, better group, who both refrain from evil and devote themselves to frequent good deeds. They understand how good it is to be sober, chaste, humble, loving toward their neighbors and faithful to prayer, and to practice the other virtues. But it is also characteristic of this group that, while they do not neglect to do what good they can, they see no need to do more than that. They do not burn with desire for a more complete holiness. So much prayer and fasting, so much keeping watch and working, so much almsgiving—this is enough for them. They remain quietly content with this spiritual level and abandon higher things to others. "So I saw that there is nothing better than that a man should enjoy his work; for that is his lot" (Eccles. 3:22).

4. Better still is the third group. They too detest and avoid wrongdoing, and fervently commit themselves to whatever good they can do. But when they have done all they can, they consider it nothing compared with what they long to do (Luke 17:10).

Knowing that "while bodily training is of some value, godliness is of value in every way" (1Tim. 4:8), they eagerly desire the spiritual and internal virtues—fondness for prayer, an intimate knowledge of God, and the experience of divine love. They believe that they are nothing and have nothing, that they obtain no comfort from earthly or heavenly things, as long as they lack opportunity to exercise these virtues and enjoy the sweetness of devotion.

This third group is not, however, inflamed with fervent zeal against the vices of others or the dangers of their sins. They want everyone to be good and live in grace, but feel no wound of sorrow when they see the opposite. They simply remain themselves intent upon God. When such persons are called to direct others, they prove little suited to the task, because they put off caring for their charges in order to preserve their own peace. "Shall I leave my sweetness and my good fruit, and go to sway over the other trees?" (Judg. 9:11).

5. The best persons for headship are those who avoid wrongdoing and practice virtue, but are also afire with zeal for righteousness and for souls. They obtain no comfort from progress toward their own salvation unless they are also leading others to God. The Lord is their example; although he always had complete joy in himself, he was not content only to possess glory, but "emptied himself, taking the form of a servant" (Phil. 2:7), in order to lead many children into glory with him through his teaching and his work.

Zeal for righteousness, like scarlet "twice dyed" (Exod. 26:1,31,36),[1] shines with the double glow of charity—love of God and of neighbor. A person who loves God not only desires to enjoy his goodness and be close to him, but loves to see his will accomplished, his worship carried out, and his honor exalted. Such persons desire everybody to know, love, serve, and honor God more than everything else. Those who love their neighbors desire not only health and prosperity for them, but, even more, eternal salvation. The more complete this charity becomes, the more fervently do we desire to help people to be saved, the more determined is our eagerness for them, and the purer our joy when

---

[1] Translated from the Vulgate.

they find salvation. For charity "does not insist on its own way" (1Cor. 13:5) but seeks what is of God.

Love God and seek the things of God single-heartedly, and you will grieve to see him dishonored and unknown, neither loved nor obeyed, his worship destroyed, his adversaries multiplied and rejoicing. To the extent that you love your neighbor's salvation, you will mourn his damnation and indeed anything harmful to him.

Righteousness

6. Although all who are God's friends have to love their neighbor too, brotherly love is especially necessary in those who serve God in religious leadership. Their position demands that they act on God's behalf, and so their hearts should be as much moved by love of righteousness and hatred of wickedness as is God's heart. "You love righteousness and hate wickedness; therefore God, your God, has anointed you" (Ps. 45:7). "Righteousness" here refers to all the qualities needed for the salvation or spiritual progress of souls.

7. In some cases the need for these qualities derives from eternal law; without humility, purity, love, mercy, and the like, no one is ever saved. The commandments of God, according to both the old and the new law, are especially directed toward these virtues: "You shall love the Lord your God with all your heart and with all your soul and with all your mind. . . . You shall love your neighbor as yourself. On these two commandments depend all the law and the prophets" (Matt. 22:37-40).

The need for some other qualities derives from human decrees, made on God's behalf by the authority of the Church and canonically established for the benefit of all. The ritual to be observed in celebrating the sacraments is a good example. Canon law says that "the decrees of the canons ought to be observed by all," whether laymen or clergy, wherever the decrees apply to their situation.

Some requirements are demanded of people through their own free act. If a person, without being under any undue influence, willingly makes a vow, the law of God demands that he or she keep it. Thus, whatever the rule of a religious order imposes, such as obedience, giving up all one's wealth, and remaining celibate, the members of the order are obliged to live up to it. "When you make a vow to the Lord your God, you shall not be slack to pay it; for the Lord your God will surely require it of you, and it would be sin in you. But if you refrain from vowing, it shall be no sin in you. You shall be careful to perform what has passed your lips, for you have voluntarily vowed to the Lord your God what you have promised with your mouth" (Deut. 23:21-23).

Other qualities that belong to righteousness have to do with the circumstances or situations in which we can make spiritual progress, although they do not refer to things necessary for salvation. Thus, there are rules about public worship and other prayers, about silence, work, food and clothing, keeping vigil and other spiritual exercises, which vary from one Christian community to another, according to what each group sees as helpful. Such exercises do not, in themselves, lead to salvation, nor does one lose one's salvation by breaking the rules concerning them. But breaking these rules does disrupt the good order of one's community and so interferes with one's own spiritual progress and with the example which one ought to give others. A person who loves righteousness will be glad to see rules of this kind faithfully kept, and will encourage it, while it will grieve and anger him to see them broken. "Do I not hate them that hate thee, O Lord? And do I not loathe them that rise against thee?" (Ps. 139:21).

Judging Wrongdoing

8. A leader's ability to judge right and wrong will increase as he deepens his awareness of serious wrongdoing and pays less attention to minor offenses. A wise man weighs all things as to their being good or bad, but a foolish man often regards serious matters as though they were trivial, and trivial as serious. To him "a speck" is like "a log" (Matt. 7:3); he has "neglected weightier matters . . . straining out a gnat and swallowing a camel" (Matt. 23:23-24). Such persons are led, not by the Spirit of God, but by their own individual eagerness. For example, some heads of communities are very fervent in correcting a single failure to bow one's head at the right moment during common prayers, but they ignore the person who regularly gossips about the faults of another

member of the community. They become more harshly indignant over the neglect of a minor ritual during prayers than over a serious and scandalous disturbance in the community.

9. The most serious forms of wrongdoing, those which we should be most careful to avoid, are those that break any commandment of God or of the Church; those that violate any serious agreement a person has voluntarily made, like observance of the rule of a religious order; and those that are likely to scandalize others by giving some appearance of evil. Signs of greed, pride, envy, gluttony, anger, disobedience, overly-intimate friendships, and other vices give Christian communities a foul reputation. "The name of God is blasphemed among the gentiles because of you" (Rom. 2:24).

People should be built up in faith by committed participants in Christian communities; they should learn from us what to do and what to avoid. They ought not to receive scandal from us, but be nourished in spirit by our good example. Even a gravely sinful action committed in secret is more easily cured than a scandal, for it may be healed by secret penance. But the effect of a scandal can hardly be extracted from the hearts of all who may have heard of it.

10. The second most serious type of wrongdoing is anything that interferes with fervent devotion. True faithfulness to religion derives from devotion, and every exercise of virtue is made fruitful by it. Religious commitment not anointed with this oil is arid. An organization devoted to good works is as unstable as a stone wall built without mortar when its participants are not joined together through frequent and fervent prayer (Ezek. 13:10-15). The lamps of the foolish virgins went out without oil (Matt. 25:1-13). In every Christian community where fervor grows tepid, actions that require other virtues begin to decline, and the community is in danger of ruin.

11. Finally, one must beware of neglecting exterior discipline, because that is a sign of a neglected conscience and interior superficiality. Rules of conduct are established to preserve the community's good order and to stabilize the spiritual progress of its members. Observance of such discipline, however, is not commanded on the grounds that it is wrong to live in any other way.

Rather, it is better suited to the character of a community for the conduct of the brethren to conform to a single pattern; if all of the members live as they wish and do as they please, they may disturb many others.

In all the details of exterior discipline, where a rule exists not to prevent evil but to support the goodness of the life of the community, a head must see to it that the rule is kept in the right spirit, faithfully but without scrupulous worry over every possible transgression. Otherwise, a custom that was originally good may give birth to a deformity, and concealment may nourish neglect. This does not mean that zeal for discipline should relax. It should, however, be forewarned against such evil consequences.

How to Deal with Wrongdoing

12. A guide who has genuine zeal for righteousness will first of all not do or teach anything evil. Secondly, he will not permit evil in his community nor concede that it is acceptable, no matter what trickery or determination is used to sway him. Third, he will never encourage evil or show pleasure in it on occasions when it has actually been done behind his back. Fourth, he will not remain silent and pretend to know nothing when he ought to speak out, show how wrong an action is, and take precautions to prevent anyone from trying to do such a thing again. Finally, he will not let bad behavior go unpunished, for the punishment of sin brings about something good. Punishment keeps an individual from falling into further sin: "Sin no more, that nothing worse befall you" (John 5:14). It cleanses the guilty person from a sin that God might otherwise punish more harshly: "If you beat him with a rod, you will save his life from Sheol" (Prov. 23:14). And the punishment teaches others to avoid similar offenses: "Strike a scoffer, and the simple will learn prudence" (Prov. 19:25). Furthermore, the leader himself, as a representative of our heavenly Judge, rescues himself from the sin of neglect by doing his duty. When the priest Eli did not do this, he brought death on himself and his two sinful sons (1Sam. 4:11ff).

13. The difference between praiseworthy Christian communities and those that have lost their fervor is not that the

praiseworthy ones have no sinful members, but that in them no one is allowed to misbehave without penalty. The gates to wrongdoing are carefully kept shut, and those who do good are shown favor and love so that they preserve and improve continually. Even the community of the angels, before they were confirmed in grace, and the apostles, with Christ as their leader, "he charges with error" (Job 4:18). What earthly body of good people would dare to claim the privilege of sinlessness for themselves? "You are clean but not all" (John 13:10); although many, through God's grace, are clear of sin, not all are.

14. In fact, the mixture of good people and bad that is found in Christian communities is beneficial. For as long as the good members are still able to practice virtue themselves, they benefit from having some bad persons living with them. The bad provide an occasion of greater merit for the good. Their own zeal must become more fervent; they must work harder to correct the others' wrongdoing; they must endure persecution from them; they will be humbled by being lumped together with them in the opinion of others; they suffer the consequences of the wrongdoers' actions along with them. They should learn to give thanks to God, who has kept them from becoming the kind of people who do evil, lest they become such. "Whatever a man sows, that he will also reap" (Gal. 6:7); if good people lack the occasions for virtue that come to them from living with the bad, to that extent their merits will be reduced.

15. Those who behave badly are not to be favored or preferred in the community, but they should be tolerated, especially when their wrongdoing is unknown and has not affected others and when there is still hope for their correction. If they do not meet these conditions, however, keeping them in the community will do serious harm. They should be expelled. Otherwise it will be supposed that the good members of the community condone their misbehavior.

Even while their misconduct is being tolerated, however, wrongdoers ought to be subjected to penalties, admonished, corrected, shamed, and punished. They should also be soothed by exhortations and words of comfort. The leader should pray with them and promise them better treatment if they recover from their moral frailty and become strong. Close every avenue of sin to them; keep temptation away from them—that is even beneficial for the good, who may be weakened by opportunities to do wrong.

The leader of a community is God's representative, "whom the Master will set over his household" (Luke 12:42); his subordinates obey him because he has the Lord's place. He will render a heavy account to the Lord if he does not correct the delinquent, if he allows vices and evil customs to grow up under his government, or lets those that have already arisen grow stronger and spread. If he sees that the kind of life required by the rule of the community is not being lived and that transgressions are becoming more numerous, he must do what he can to overcome both the present evils and those that threaten.

16. Leaders who neglect these duties will render account to God on three points.

First, they were neglectful in not doing what duty required. "Because as servants of his kingdom you did not rule rightly, nor keep the law, nor walk according to the purpose of God, he will come upon you terribly and swiftly, because severe judgment falls on those in highest places" (Wis. 6:5-6).

Second, they bear the guilt for all the faults of their subordinates, because they could and should have corrected them and issued warnings about them. "If I say to the wicked, O wicked man, you shall surely die, and you do not speak to warn the wicked to turn from his way, that wicked man shall die in his iniquity, but his blood I will require at your hand" (Ezek. 33:8).

Third, they have abused the honor and the power that belong to their positions by perverting them to their own glory and advantage, rather than employing them in their true purpose. "Take the talent from him . . . and cast the worthless servant into the outer darkness; there men will weep and gnash their teeth" (Matt. 25:28-30).

17. But a good director, zealous for righteousness, shows how much he loves God by doing the will of God himself and by fostering submission to God's will in others. His zeal does not grow tame in idleness, nor does his labor wear him out. Bad advice does not turn him from the right path, nor does trickery get around him. Neither friendship nor flattery change his purpose, nor do threats

scare him. He does not lose hope, even when he must confront the same bad habits every day, but sticks to his task.

Chapter Three

Brotherly Love

1. The second quality that one who is in charge of a Christian community needs is brotherly love, or compassion. Just as the love of God inflames his zeal for righteousness, affection for his brethren should form him in brotherly love. "Thy rod and thy staff they comfort me" (Ps. 23:5). "What do you wish? Shall I come to you with a rod, or with love in a spirit of gentleness?" (1Cor. 4:21). Let the rod strike down vice; it is just as necessary for the staff to sustain weakness.

The good Samaritan, finding the victim of the bandits lying abandoned and only half alive, poured oil and wine on his wounds (Luke 10:33). When a member of the community needs help, the guide should offer the wine of fervent zeal and the oil of comforting brotherly love.

2. Both physical and mental weaknesses may affect the members of a Christian community. The weaknesses are different, but each needs our compassion.

Physical Weakness

Physical infirmities take three forms. First come those who are bedridden with chronic or acute illnesses. Then there are the housebound and others who can walk outside from time to time, but suffer from chronic disabling conditions. Lastly, some are frail and worn out from age or exhausting work, although they have no definite illness, or they are constitutionally prone to temporary weariness and sickness.

A loving director will provide help for these afflicted individuals in three ways: by getting appropriate medical attention for them; by reducing the austerity of their lives with respect to fasts, vigils, garb, and the like; and by exempting them to whatever extent is necessary from the tasks, services, studies, and so on to which the members of the community are ordinarily obliged. According to the need of each, let the head provide remedies for the most urgent needs first.

3. One must show every kindness to the sick and enfeebled, because they are suffering at the Lord's hands. If, on top of that, they endure tribulation from men, their very misery will cry aloud to the Father of mercies against those who trouble them: "They persecute him whom thou hast smitten, and him whom thou hast wounded they afflict still more" (Ps. 69:26). A sick person cannot help himself in his afflicted condition and is all the more troubled if those who are committed to him do not console him, relieve him from his work, provide for his needs, or have compassion on him. "Insults have broken my heart, so that I am in despair. I looked for pity, but there was none; and for comforters, but I found none. They gave me poison for food, and for my thirst they gave me vinegar to drink" (Ps. 69:20-21).

4. A good leader knows that he is the father, not the lord, of his brothers, and shows himself their physician, rather than their tyrant. He does not think of them as cattle or slaves to be purchased, but as sons and fellow heirs with him of a supernatural inheritance. He should treat them as he wishes others to treat him were he in the same need (Matt. 7:12). Strong, healthy people do not have the same feelings as the invalid; they do not know how to appreciate their sufferings. They will understand later when they have pains of their own.

Some may object that the sick often pretend to be more enfeebled than they are, and therefore suggest that they should be treated as hypocrites. The Lord, on the contrary, chose to spare many evil men for the sake of the few righteous (Gen. 18:23-33). The good leaders will do their best for all the sick, those who complain too much along with the rest.

5. There are three reasons why the infirm need more loving help than the healthy and robust. First, they cannot obtain by themselves the necessities of life. If they do not receive physical sustenance from others, they cannot survive. "Take care to prevent the enfeebled one from perishing" (2 Sam. 14:14).[1]

---

[1] This is an idiomatic translation of the actual Latin text. The RSV version is hard to understand, does not translate the Vulgate text used by the author, and does not fit the context.

Second, in their infirmity they have lost their health and strength. Those who are healthy and strong need sustenance only in order to keep what they have. The sick and weak need help for two purposes: to avoid losing whatever strength they still have, and to recover what they have lost. "From him who has not, even what he has will be taken away" (Luke 19:26).

Finally, the help they receive is itself a relief for their troubles. For it comforts them in their many afflictions to see that others have compassion for them and can be counted on to assist them in their efforts at recovery. "May you be blessed by the Lord; for you have had compassion on me" (1Sam. 23:21).

6. Some say that it is proper to help invalids who have some hope of recovery, but a useless expense in cases where no recovery can be expected. There would be point to that argument if the merciful love that one owes to the infirm were based on human advantages and not on the value of divine love. In fact, a person who takes care of the infirm in order to be repaid after they recover health deprives himself of the merit of charity (Luke 6:34-35). The more generous our mercy and the more unselfish our charity, the more clearly do we show ourselves to be merciful and charitable, rather than calculating.

"We have not a high priest who is unable to sympathize with our weaknesses" (Heb. 4:15). It is even beneficial for the head to experience the same infirmities as the rest sometimes, for he learns to have compassion on them.

Spiritual Weakness

7. Spiritual infirmities also fall into three categories. Lack of spiritual commitment, or an impulsive yielding to temptation, makes some individuals prone to scandalous behavior, wrongdoing, vacillation from good courses to evil, and a tendency to lapses. "Many of you are weak and ill" (1Cor. 11:30).

There are others who are devout and well-intentioned but weak. A mild disagreement or, still more, a strong objection hinders them from doing the good they desire. Then they either become hopelessly discouraged or so angry as to cause a serious commotion. Later they are sorry, but others in the community have been disturbed: "We who are strong ought to bear with the failings of the weak" (Rom. 15:1).

Finally there are many imperfect persons who vacillate in their efforts to be virtuous. They feel in themselves, even if unwillingly, the fevers of the passions—anger, laziness, self-exaltation, pride, lust, and other fleshly and spiritual vices. "Be gracious to me, O Lord, for I am languishing" (Ps. 6:2).

8. Three remedies must be provided for these failings. First, deny such people any opportunity to give scandal or do wrong. To keep them from hearing or seeing anything that may weaken their wills, prevent them from often going out on their own away from the community.

Next, give them a good example of patience, and at the same time keep up their courage by frequent exhortations. Until they recover from their infirmities, spare them from harsh rebukes and any other treatment which might further offend or distress them. "Do not provoke your children, lest they become discouraged" (Col. 3:21). Indeed, giving further disturbance to an already disturbed person is like provoking a barking dog into biting.

Finally, learn to put up with their minor imperfections and personal habits without becoming disturbed, recognizing that we cannot all do everything (Sir. 17:30).

9. Learned individuals are lenient toward mistakes made by the ignorant and unskilled; so too, people of tried virtue kindly put up with the defects of others, knowing that everyone cannot be equally perfect. They do not burden those who are young and immature in Christ with more than they can endure, nor do they demand of them what exceeds their strength. "My lord knows that the children are frail, and that the flocks and herds giving suck are a care to me; and if they are overdriven for one day, all the flocks will die" (Gen. 33:13). These immature little ones have definite good will; but do not drive them to conform to a stricter standard of virtue than they have the grace for. That will extinguish what grace they have by making them more agitated than their spiritual strength can sustain. "We were gentle among you, like a nurse taking care of her children" (1Thess. 2:7); that is to say, I am humble, kind and mild with you, asking no more than the weak and imperfect can do.

Brotherly Love

The Lord has a quarrel with shepherds who are harsh and lack compassion: "The weak you have not strengthened, the sick you have not healed, the crippled you have not bound up, the strayed you have not brought back, the lost you have not sought, and with force and harshness you have ruled them" (Ezek. 34:4). Bernard of Clairvaux says, "Learn how to be mothers to those under your headship, not lords; study how to be loved rather than feared. If at times only severity can do the job, let it be not a tyrant's but a father's severity. Prove yourselves to be mothers by the way you foster those under your care; by the way you correct them prove that you are fathers. Be mild, not harsh; restrain yourself from blows, and offer comfort. Be filled with the milk of human kindness, not swollen with rage. Why make your yoke weigh so heavy upon them, when you should be carrying their burdens?"[2] "Carry them in your bosom, as a nurse carries a suckling child, to the land which thou didst swear to give their fathers" (Num. 11:12).

---

[2] *On the Song of Songs*, Sermon 23, n. 2.

Chapter Four

Patience

1. The third virtue required in a leader is unwavering patience, or long-suffering. In order to keep the interior of the temple clean, there had to be a roof to bear dust, rain, and gusts of wind (Exod. 26:7; 35:11). In the same way, leaders faithfully defend those under their direction from the storms of sin. To do so, they must often expose themselves to the force of various adversities, as a mother hen will battle a bird of prey to protect her children.

The Need for Patience

2. There are three principal reasons why the guide needs a great deal of patience. First, many responsibilities, time-consuming activities, and fatiguing tasks demand his attention. For he is responsible for both the spiritual and physical welfare of the members of the community. We see that Paul was anxious to meet not only the spiritual, but also the temporal needs of the faithful, especially of the poor: "James and Cephas and John . . . would have us remember the poor, which very thing I was eager to do" (Gal. 2:9-10). The Lord himself fed those who had received the word of salvation with ordinary bread that they needed but could not obtain (Mark 6:35-44; 8:1-10).

The many time-consuming activities of headship derive from both the community's internal concerns and its dealings with the outside. To some extent, a leader must take thought for these things even if it causes him anxiety, for he is the person responsible for them.

The fatiguing tasks of headship include business dealings, journeys, and other jobs that will often keep one busy late into the night, demanding much patience. Moses, meek and close to God as he was, wanted to give up the burden of governing Israel on this account, for he felt unable to handle the task. "How can I bear alone the weight and burden of you and your strife? Choose wise, understanding, and experienced men according to your tribes, and I will appoint them as your heads" (Deut. 1:12-13).

3. A leader also needs patience when he sees how little return he gets for all his labor. For even though he wears himself out, he will not see much spiritual growth in the community. He may try many things and finally, after much labor, find the people under him beginning to improve a little. But so many obstacles stand in the way of spiritual progress that they will easily be delayed again. A leader may be tempted to despair of ever seeing a return for his labors; he is like a farmer who sows much but reaps a poor harvest (Hag. 1:6).

At times, a director will even see that rules he personally established are neglected and that his orders are carelessly obeyed. Often he will find evil conduct stealing into the community under the appearance of good. Something will appear to be good, so that he dares not denounce it as evil, but in reality it destroys some greater good and opens the door for more obvious evils.

For example, a sincere desire to save many souls may lead a community to accept more members than it can properly manage. That very multiplication of its numbers then hinders the community's observance of poverty. More of the members will want to enjoy more good things rather than live simply. From that follow more frequent business dealings to acquire the necessities of life. Soon the community is trying unusual methods for raising money and accepting gifts that the rule prohibits. Thus, the peace of a devout life disappears, while the community's religious standards lie neglected. The members begin aimlessly traveling around, hunting out various provisions for the flesh (Rom. 13:14). They enter relationships prohibited by the rule; they look for gifts from those who seek their advice; they curry favor with the rich. They give up tasks that would strengthen other Christians in return for opportunities to beg. They expand their properties, build sumptuous residences, but do not cure scandals. Such activities crush the honor of God underfoot—that honor which a community ought to advance by its holy conduct and the inspiration it gives to its neighbors. A similar abuse occurs when young men, and men whose virtue has not been seriously tested, are prematurely ordained or given responsibility for community leadership, preaching, and counseling.

In short, many things can be done that look good to human opinion, but actually stain our once pure interior devotion to God. Some people in the community, being dull and imperceptive about the interior life, may even suppose that all the power of a spiritual way of life lies in the external appearance of greatness. Accordingly, they defend such practices with great zeal, while neglecting true virtues and genuinely spiritual matters.

These and similar abuses will cause a spirit-filled leader profound disappointment and pain. Since he is unable to correct all these problems even though he longs to do so, he has great need of patience. "My zeal consumes me. . ." (Ps. 119:139). "Zeal for thy house has consumed me. . ."(Ps. 69:9).

4. A third reason why a leader needs patience is the ungratefulness of those he works and cares for. His charges are scarcely ever satisfied with him; rather, they always feel put upon, because they are sure that he could do things differently, and better, if he wished. Often one is perplexed, not knowing whether to yield to their constant demands and allow everything they want, or to hold firmly to the course of action that one believes will do more good: "Which I shall choose I cannot tell. I am hard pressed between the two" (Phil. 1:22-23).

Many things that a leader does are twisted by his people and given a bad interpretation. They murmur at his decisions, make accusations against him, reveal his faults, and derive matter for scandal from things that he did out of a sense of duty to God and to them. It is almost impossible to escape the fact that whatever one determines or does, it will upset some of the members of the community. Some will go so far as to resist their leader to his face or argue with him in writing. They scorn him and rouse others to oppose him, or else find clever ways to keep him from fulfilling his duties.

The Shield of Patience

5. To stand up against these conflicts, and others which will confront him, a leader needs a shield of threefold patience. First,

he must know how to answer everyone modestly, maturely, and kindly, so that he can stop overheated attacks without showing impatience in his speech or expression—without, in fact, even developing an impatient outlook. His patience will gain him more ground and finally win over those who would only be further provoked by impetuous action. Thus Gideon gave a modest answer when the men of Ephraim reproached him and so pacified the bitter anger stirring within them (Judg. 8:1-3). "A soft answer turns away wrath, but a harsh word stirs up anger" (Prov. 15:1). After all, a disturbance will hardly be calmed by further disturbance, nor does one vice cure another.

A leader who does become impatient upsets the good he could have achieved. Impatience has a number of bad results. It scandalizes others: "He who has a hasty temper exalts folly" (Prov. 14:29). It renders a person contemptible to those in his charge and to other people as well: "The one of perverse mind is despised" (Prov. 12:8). It makes a person hateful and dreaded: "A man who is reckless in speech will be hated" (Sir. 9:18).

Impatience also provokes others to impatience: "The hot-tempered man stirs up strife, but he who is slow to anger quiets contention" (Prov. 15:18). It makes the members of the community afraid to go to the leader with their needs: "If one ventures a word with you, will you be offended?" (Job 4:2). As a result, the community is filled with murmuring and rancor: "He who troubles his household will inherit the wind" (Prov. 11:29), "wind" meaning "conspiracies." An impatient leader scares off the simple members and makes them timid.[1] Then no one will dare to warn him when something requires correction: "He is so ill-natured that one cannot speak to him" (1Sam. 25:17).

6. Next, a head of a community should try to be a peacemaker—the second way in which patience is a shield. He should not avenge injuries done to him, nor hate those who inflict the injuries, nor hesitate to work for their cure. He should be glad to keep ungrateful persons in the community, for he will strengthen both these and other members by so doing good to them. He himself will grow in virtue through such persons, as our supreme Shepherd says:

---

[1] The author quotes Prov. 18:14, which in the Vulgate, because of an error, reads, "Who can endure the spirit of one who is easily angered?"

"You will be sons of the Most High, for he is kind to the ungrateful and the selfish" (Luke 6:35).

Leaders should not try to separate such people from themselves. It is, after all, the shepherd's chief duty to teach virtuous living. What good will it do to remove from his care the very people who most need his help? If the doctor runs away from the sick, who will heal them? If a soldier shuns the attack, how will he taste victory? If business managers neglect the deals which offer most profit, how will they get rich? This is the reason why many bishops, pastors, and religious superiors become saints: the nature of their duties gives them opportunity to do much good, to suffer many adversities, and to lead others to the heights of perfection. "If anyone aspires to the office of bishop, he desires a noble task" (1Tim. 3:1).

7. The third aspect of the shield of patience is perseverance. Whatever his difficulties, the leader must be willing and eager to do everything that his duties require. Sometimes this work is exhausting, its progress is slow, the members of the community are demanding, and there are other burdens. Yet all these obstacles can lead to high merit. "But you, take courage! Do not let your hands be weak, for your work shall be rewarded" (2Chron. 15:7). The "hands" of a leader are determination in getting his job done and patience in bearing burdens. If they are not weakened by laziness or impatience, their eternal reward will constantly increase.

8. The adversities that a guide undergoes can actually carry several advantages. For one thing, if his human weakness has entangled him in wrongdoing, his hardships cleanse him of its effects. "For we all make many mistakes" (James 3:2). Where there is much to do, much is often neglected. Leaders, therefore, need to be cleansed here, so that they need not he punished hereafter. "When he commits iniquity, I will chasten him with the rod of men, with the stripes of the sons of men" (2 Sam. 7:14).

9. Adversity also protects one from the swelling of pride, which is more insidious for those in authority. The high position, the extent of one's freedom, and the gratification of doing good work might easily make one proud. But the yoke of adversity bows down the neck of presumption and thus defends the leader from the yawning gulf of pride. "Then he opens the ears of men, that he may

turn man aside from his deed, and cut off pride from man; he keeps back his soul from the Pit, his life from perishing by the sword. Man is also chastened with pain upon his bed, and with continual strife in his bones" (Job 33:16-19).

A good guide's own salvation and spiritual progress are protected by humbling adversity; without it, success would lift him up on the wind of presumption. David, a man after God's own heart, was humble and very fervent as long as he was hard pressed by trouble: "It is good for me that I was afflicted, that I might learn thy statutes" (Ps. 119:71). But when prosperity raised him up, he fell into sin.

10. A leader's holiness, as we said before, increases through both the good he does and the evil he suffers. It is glorious to do good and to inspire others to do good. To suffer adversities leads to a magnificent crown, as gold that is tried in the fire becomes more beautiful and more precious.

In fact, spiritual progress is often made when one does not feel the increase, and one is strengthened while seeming to grow more infirm. "The kingdom of God is as if a man should scatter seed upon the ground, and should sleep and rise night and day, and the seed should sprout and grow, he knows not how" (Mark 4:26-27).

It is little wonder that not all the efforts of a guide lead to profit for everyone; even God, who works in all people, does not succeed in bringing about the salvation of every human being. "Many are called but few are chosen" (Matt. 22:14). Not every seed that is sown comes to fruition, and those who dig for treasure willingly tear up large tracts of land to find a little gold and silver. The true effect of a good director can be measured by the amount of harm that would befall the community without him. Direction is like light, so good to have that its mere absence is an evil.

This truth should encourage the person who guides a community to bear up under his work load, for he serves God just as faithfully in giving leadership to those who make little or no progress as in giving it to those who do the best. "Each shall receive his wages according to his labor" (1Cor. 3:8), and it is "only God who gives the growth" (1Cor. 3:7). Just as goods that are much harder to make sell for more, so a farmer who labors over sterile and rocky soil gets only a small crop, but can often ask a higher price. A teacher, too, works harder with a pupil who will not learn than with one who will, and so, in all such cases, to a just judge, their labors are more meritorious.

Chapter Five

Good Example

1. The life of the leader should be a model to the rest of the community. What his words teach his actions ought to show, as the diagrams drawn by a geometry teacher illustrate his proofs. "Jesus began to do and teach" (Acts 1:1). "I have given you an example, that you also should do as I have done to you" (John 13:15). "Look at me, and do likewise" (Judg. 7:17).

The guide of a Christian community should give an example of all the virtues to the people under his authority. There are three ways in which he can give such an example: by conforming himself to the observance of everything that makes up the community's life, by humbly showing kindness to all people, and by conducting himself with mature honesty. "Show yourself in all respects a model of good deeds, and in your teaching show integrity, gravity and sound speech that cannot be censured" (Titus 2:7-8).

Observing the Common Life

2. The first of the three ways to give good example is by sharing the same standard of living as the rest of the community with respect to clothing, food, and work. The leader ought not to relax with a nice drink among his guests while everyone else is restricted to plain food and beverages. Nor should he dress differently from the rest, since he shares with them the same commitment. As the one who directs the members of a community in their daily work, he ought not to avoid taking a share in it. For if the shepherd cuts himself out of the flock, he exposes the sheep to the tricks of the wolves.

Instead, the shepherd should be strong with the strong and weak with the weak: "To the weak I became weak, as an example for them, that I might win the weak. I have become all things to all men, that I might by all means save some" (1Cor. 9:22). For if a strong man lives as though he were frail, other strong people in the community follow his example and begin to indulge the flesh. But if a sick man refuses to take appropriate remedies, he intimidates other sick people by suggesting either that he wants them to do likewise, or that he does not desire their recovery. A soldier is more quick to the battle line if he sees his leader enduring the toil of the struggle along with him.

The apostles were aware of the importance of our Lord's example to them "during all the time that the Lord Jesus went in and out among us, beginning from the baptism of John until the day when he was taken up from us" (Acts 1:21-22). That is, from the time that the Lord first took disciples after his baptism, right up until the moment he ascended to the Father, he always taught them by his own example. "He went in," living with his disciples as his family, and "he went out," giving valuable teachings to the crowds that gathered.

Humility

3. It is also important for the leader to be humble in his conduct. Let his behavior show that he does not think too highly of himself, nor assumes the airs of an official. It should be clear that he fears his role, that he retains his responsibilities because he is required to do so, and would prefer to be subordinate rather than to rule. He should also show that he considers those in his charge better than himself, and would rather regard himself as a servant than as a lord or master. "Let the greatest among you become as the youngest, and the leader as one who serves..." (Luke 22:26-27). "I am among you as one who serves. If they make you master of the feast, do not exalt yourself; be among them as one of them" (Sir. 32:1).

4. A humble man sees to it that members of the community have ready access to him. He is pleasant-spoken, so that they can discuss their needs with him trustfully. He listens patiently, does every kindness he can, and offers careful instruction and prompt exhortation. He should take pains to be more loved than feared, because a beloved leader is more willingly obeyed. Loving obedience is characteristically voluntary, while fearful obedience derives from compulsion. The more voluntary our obedience, the higher its merit. Since a faithful guide wants his people to develop such merits, he

should seek for willing obedience. After all, the purpose of spiritual authority is to direct those in one's charge toward eternal life.

5. The leader ought to show humility in his use of property and goods, neither having nor seeking luxuries. Everything he owns should show his willing acceptance of poverty and so reveal his humility. This applies to his home and room, to his furniture and appliances, his books, clothing, food and table, and whatever else he has. Nothing he owns should be showy or interesting just as a curiosity, nor should he let others in his community keep such things. For like enjoys like: lofty men delight in sublimities, but lowly men delight in lowly things. It is no sign of a humble heart to seek out curiosities, or to be ambitious to own and show off what is precious and luxurious. "He beholds everything that is high; he is king over all the sons of pride" (Job 41:34).

Maturity

6. There are three ways a leader can show his maturity. First, he should never act lightly. Thus, he avoids jokes and phrases that seem funny but are really hurtful or silly. People neither admire nor respect those who habitually indulge in such false humor. As Pope Gregory the Great observed, "It is hard to accept the preaching of someone who behaves like a trifler."[1] While a leader should usually be more loved than feared, it is good for the insolent person to feel some fear toward him. Love itself is felt more strongly when combined with reverence as is evident in our love for our Creator: the more we acknowledge his absolute majesty, the better do we love his sweet condescension. "Good and upright is the Lord; therefore he instructs sinners in the way" (Ps. 25:8).

7. Also, the leader ought not to be light with his affections. He must discipline himself to avoid wrong sexual attachments or any kind of significant involvement with anyone whose character is questionable. The more faithful members of the community are to be preferred in one's affections, and everyone should be embraced in one's hope for their salvation in Christ.

---

[1] *Homilies on Ezekiel*, 1, sermon 3, n. 4.

A leader's conduct should be such that all the members of the community trust him and confide in him as their best friend, each one taking his love for granted. He should do nothing to cause a person to feel scorned, nor should he arbitrarily prefer one person over another. "Joseph's brothers hated him just because their father had such a special love for him" (Gen. 37); never show such favoritism as to nourish indignation or envy in others.

8. Finally, a leader should not lightly change his plans for action or his advice. Suppose that something pleases him at one moment and displeases him the next, or that he wants one thing now and later the contrary. After seeing such lack of stability, who will accept his judgment or adapt to his will? Under such circumstances, his subordinates cannot respect his prudence, nor commit themselves to obey his direction. The resulting damage may be serious. "Do all things without grumbling or questioning" (Phil. 2:14), that is without hesitating and reconsidering. "Test everything; hold fast what is good" (1Thess. 5:21).

One may, of course, have good reason to alter some decisions out of real necessity or some solid religious advantage. Such changes are not a sign of levity but of maturity. It would be stupid to give up the better for the sake of the worse; it would likewise be sheer obstinacy to stick to one's first plans so stubbornly that even a great and obvious benefit could not bring one to change them. "We will take care to render our kingdom quiet and peaceable for all men, by changing our methods and always judging what comes before our eyes with more equitable consideration" (Est. 16:8-9).

When Paul excused himself from his promise to visit the Corinthians, he assured them that he had not changed his mind lightly, but for their own sake: "I wanted to come to you first, so that you might have a double pleasure. . . . Was I vacillating when I wanted to do this? Do I make my plans like a worldly man, ready to say yes and no at once? As surely as God is faithful, our word to you has not been yes and no. . . . But I call God to witness against me—it was to spare you that I refrained from coming to Corinth" (2Cor. 1:15-23).

The leader, both when upholding his previous decisions and when changing them for good reason, must bear this in mind: "Like the magistrate of the people, so are his officials; and like the ruler of the city, so are all its inhabitants" (Sir. 10:2).

The Value of Example

9. Good masters generally form good disciples. People who see a better way of living exemplified by their instructors often become better Christians and better participants in the community's life. The leader who neglects his duty to give a good example will be strictly judged: "Thus says the Lord God: Behold, I am against the shepherds. I will require my sheep at their hand, and put a stop to their feeding the sheep; no longer shall the shepherds feed themselves. I will rescue my sheep from their mouths, that they may not be food for them" (Ezek. 34:10).

Verbal instruction unaccompanied by active good example is like mortar without lime—dry and without strength. "And I will break down the wall that you have daubed with whitewash, and bring it down to the ground, so that its foundation will be laid bare; when it falls, you shall perish in the midst of it; and you shall know that I am the Lord" (Ezek. 13:14). A new edition of a book can only be as correct as the older copy on which it is based. Actions speak louder than words; the lessons we teach are more firmly embedded in our deeds than in our speech. "A man's preaching is despised if his way of life is worthy of scorn."[2]

The director ought to commit himself with special determination to form those in his charge according to the pattern of Christ. This means that he imprints on them the way of life and the doctrine of Christ. He seeks to lead them to imitate the Lord in every aspect of their lives, not just to refer to him in their thoughts (Eph. 5:1). "Be imitators of God, as beloved children. My little children, with whom I am again in travail until Christ be formed in you" (Gal. 4:19). But verbal instruction by itself is not enough to convey the whole teaching of Christ.

Leaders, therefore, should be visible models of Christ's way of life, so that they can imprint it more deeply on their people. "Be imitators of me, as I am of Christ" (1Cor. 11:1). That is to say, if you want to be molded into the form of Christ, look carefully at my

---

[2]Gregory the Great, *Homilies on Ezekiel*, I, sermon 12, n. 1.

way of life: "It is no longer I who live, but Christ who lives in me" (Gal. 2:20). For the head of the community does indeed rule in the place of Christ; he ought to promote whatever is pleasing to Christ, exercise Christ's authority, and be himself a model of likeness to Christ.

In this way, a leader should encourage those in his charge to do the Lord's will. With the Lord's authority, he should serve his people in everything that will benefit them, and make his own life an example that they may safely imitate. "For what we preach is not ourselves, but Jesus Christ as Lord, with ourselves as your servants for Jesus' sake" (2Cor. 4:5). When the speech of a guide promotes his own glory, he preaches himself, not Christ. When he gives an example of bad conduct, he encourages his charges to imitate him rather than Christ. "They make much of you, but for no good purpose; they want to shut you out, that you may make much of them" (Gal. 4:17). This means that directors whose evil examples shut you out from the imitation of Christ act from no good motive. They want you to learn to follow their own wrong way of life.

Chapter Six

Good Judgment

1. Discernment—the ability to make prudent judgments on all actions—is the fifth virtue needed for spiritual leadership. Solomon shows how urgent is the need of it. When God offered to give him whatever he asked for, he ignored every other possibility to ask for wisdom. Without it, he declared, no king could rule his people well. "Give thy servant therefore an understanding mind to govern thy people, that I may discern between good and evil; for who is able to govern this thy great people?" (1Kings 3:9). "To you then, O monarchs, my words are directed, that you may learn wisdom and not transgress" (Wis. 6:9). "Now therefore, O kings, be wise; be warned, O rulers of the earth" (Ps. 2:10).

A director is the leader of the flock committed to his charge. If he goes off the right path, his flock will scatter in confusion. As the eye is the light of the whole body, so is the shepherd to the flock committed to him: "You are the light of the world" (Matt. 5:14). Depending on whether the eye sees clearly or badly, the body will be guided in a straight or weaving path.

2. A guide needs good judgment or discernment in order to know what to do and how to do it. For even if an activity is good in itself it will only do good when it fits the circumstances. Bernard of Clairvaux says, "Remove good judgment and virtue will become vice."[1] And indeed, without discretion, zeal turns into immature and headstrong rashness: "They have a, zeal for God, but it is not enlightened" (Rom. 10:2). Compassion, under the appearance of brotherly love, declines into sentimentality: "He who spares the rod hates his son, but he who loves him is diligent to discipline him" (Prov. 13:24). This means that any leader who fails to correct sinful behavior because he wants to show compassion is actually sending a soul to destruction.

---

[1] *Sermons on the Song of Songs*, 49, n. 5.

Without good judgment, patience robs authority of its proper vigor, so that a leader supposedly acting out of humility fails to stop rebellion: "Rehoboam was young and irresolute and could not withstand them" (2Chron. 13:7), "them" being the men who opposed his rule and God's. Even good example loses its power to build up other Christians unless it is given with discretion, just as good food needs salt for better taste. So do what good you can, but show good judgment in how, when, where, and why you do it.

3. So many problems demand good judgment in a guide that one cannot treat them all in a brief discussion. There are, however, four areas that especially require care. Provide well for these, and difficulties arising from indiscretion will be few. The first is governing those committed to one's charge in a way that will help them continue to do good and advance in holiness. The second is correcting lapsed and misbehaving members so that they return to better courses. The third is taking care of business and administrative matters and all the outside affairs in which headship involves one. And the fourth is governing oneself and providing for one's own spiritual needs in the midst of other responsibilities.

When a leader accepts responsibility to care for the souls of others, he becomes like the high priest of the Old Testament, ministering to the Lord in the sanctuary. The high priest wore a "breastplate of judgment" embellished with four rows of jewels (Exod. 28:15). The four ways in which leaders must show their good judgment are like these rows of jewels. Their fourfold discretion equips them to serve God in a task greatly pleasing to him, one that furthers the salvation of souls. For no sacrifice is more pleasing to God than zeal for souls.

Helping People Continue in Christian Life

4. A guide who sets out to help people go on living a good Christian life needs a thorough acquaintance with their habits, abilities, and consciences[2] so that he can assign each person to an appropriate place in the life of the community. For all things are not equally

---

[2] In speaking here of knowing the consciences of the brothers, the author means that the head of a Christian community should know what sort of life each has lived and should acquaint himself with their standards of morality and their conduct.

possible for everyone, "but each has his own special gift from God, one of one kind and one of another" (1Cor. 7:7).

Leaders of communities and other individuals with pastoral duties are like the high priest Aaron and his sons: "Aaron and his sons shall go in and appoint them each to his task and to his burden" (Num. 4:19). They ought to know the interior state of all those for whom they are responsible, so that they can assign duties and situations appropriate to each. This work can be divided according to three levels of importance.

5. The high priest's breastplate had four rows of jewels, with three jewels in each row. Just as the four rows can be taken as symbolic of the four duties of leadership that call for good judgment, so also the three precious stones in each row can represent three different levels of vigilance needed in fulfilling these duties.

The first degree of vigilance is called for when one is dealing with basic commitments made by members of the community, especially those serious enough to require faithfulness at any cost. The head of a Christian community has no authority to dispense the members from commitments that they have made to the Lord so solemnly that their very salvation now depends on keeping them. And the head is just as strictly obliged to keep such vows as any other member.

An example of a very serious vow would be any commitment which, if deliberately broken, would separate either the community or the individual member from Christ. Another would be anything that so changes the life of the body that the members no longer give the Lord the kind of service which they had promised. It is deadly sin to break such vows. Thus, members of religious orders who have made permanent vows of obedience, poverty, and chastity may not be dispensed from them.[3]

The leader of a Christian community must be always watchful of such commitments. All the members ought to fulfill them with zeal, but the commitments must be kept even if people are reluctant to do so. The head must enforce the observance of serious vows as

---

[3] The author here speaks of the vows of religious orders as irrevocable. This view, customary in his day, is, of course, no longer held by the Catholic Church. Also, when the author speaks of the community's commitment to give the Lord a particular type of service, he is not speaking of the kind of jobs at which community members work, but of commitments to a way of life that enables the community to offer its service.

fully as possible and may not allow them to be broken for any reason, even if this insistence brings great tribulation and loss upon the whole community. "Who shall separate us from the love of Christ? Shall tribulation, or distress, or persecution, or famine, or nakedness, or peril, or sword?" (Rom. 8:35). Paul intends us to answer: "None of these."

This is the answer for those who say, "How can we sustain ourselves, how can our brethren obtain the necessities of life, when we must follow so strict a rule?" For some ways of making a living are so contradictory to the life that we promised to live for God and bring so much disrepute upon the community that it is better for people to leave the community than support themselves by those means. If those who cannot or will not live according to the community principles depart, they do not destroy their own souls, but they do cease to scandalize others. We read in Scripture: "Whoever causes one of these little ones who believe in me to sin, it would be better for him to have a great millstone fastened round his neck and to be drowned in the depth of the sea" (Matt. 18:6). If the Lord considers it so evil to lead one person into sin, what is to be thought of those who tempt many?

Considerations regarding the community's solemn commitments are always to be borne in mind more carefully than any others. The leader, like the high priest with the most precious of his jewels, must protect these commitments above all.

6. The second aspect of the task of maintaining Christians in a good state is encouragement to go on to perfection. A director should encourage those committed to his charge to strive for the highest levels of patience, humility, love, and the other virtues; to be strict and simple in all their use of material goods; and to be fair and moderate in their response even to very trying circumstances. He should exhort, warn, and advise his people; his good example should attract and attach them to these virtues. This is better than trying to force them to live up to some very high standard of conduct. The counsels of perfection[4] are recommendations; one persuades but does not order people to follow them.

---

[4] By "counsels of perfection" the author, along with other Christian writers of his time, meant specific commitments to the closest and most faithful discipleship, through vows of poverty, celibacy, and obedience. To "follow the life of the counsels" normally required that one join a religious order.

Only when someone has bound himself by a vow (for example, a vow of sexual continence) does the observance of one of the counsels become obligatory.

The monastic life and other forms of Christian community have been established primarily as training schools in the exercises of perfection. Training and exercise for athletic contests involve strict self-denial, a fact which Paul employs as an image of the Christian struggle: "Every athlete exercises self-control in all things" (1Cor. 9:25). In Paul's day, athletes who wrestled in the gymnasium stripped their bodies entirely and covered themselves with oil so that their opponents could get no grasp to throw them for a fall. That is a good image for the Christian who seeks perfection: give up everything by which the enemy of souls can get a hold on you. Add to your belongings only what will make you more successful in the struggle.

The director, therefore, should also carry this hope in his heart, like a jewel on the high priest's breast: to teach and inspire the Lord's people not only to hold to the way of salvation, but also to direct themselves to a more perfect life. This will lead him and them to the glory of heaven.

7. A third level of vigilance in exercising good judgment is needed in determining how strictly the rules of the community should be kept. These rules help one to live and grow in God's grace, but are not in themselves essential to salvation or perfection. The founders of our communities established rules to train us in good deeds, to make our communities good and happy places to live in, and to build up those who become familiar with our lives. These are the reasons for requiring fasts, times of silence, solemn forms of public worship, and other external practices which manifest our interior commitment. "While bodily training is of some value, godliness is of value in every way" (1Tim. 4:8). The exercises that Paul recommends here are useful in the way that tools are for an artisan. Experts can do more with tools than beginners; but if need be they can even do much without them, since their craftsmanship does not depend on the use of any particular tool.

When the need arises or a greater good can be served, a leader may at his own discretion dispense those under him from obligations imposed by the rule of the community. This applies to regulations about times and places for work, prayer, and various community activities. There should be no difficulty in dispensing with such matters when a really good reason exists. On the other hand, when neither the greater good nor real necessity demands that allowances be made, he should be firm in seeing that the rules are kept.

In decisions of this nature a leader needs plenty of good judgment to know how to hold to a middle line between strictness and laxity. Excessively strict rule weakens the love that members of the community have for their guide, so that when he asks them to comply with rules in areas where compliance is indeed much needed, or very useful, they do not do so with a good will. If, however, he is too lenient, even greater troubles will follow, and discipline in the community will fail completely. "He who despises small things will fail little by little" (Sir. 19:1).

Correcting Misbehavior

8. A second range of responsibilities that require the leader's good judgment relates to the correction of misbehavior. There are three different types of offender, and a leader's discretion is tested in determining how to bring each type back into conformity with the life of the community.

Some are ready to repent as soon as they have done anything seriously wrong. They find the remedy of penance, either through external human correction or through an internal change prompted by the Holy Spirit. With this group, the spiritual physician ought to employ the medicine of mercy. The offender should indeed act to remove whatever scandal he has given others and to repent to God for his sin. His penance ought to be severe enough to deter others from doing as he has done, but easy enough to bear that he will not regret having submitted to it. "If a man is overtaken in any trespass, you who are spiritual should restore him in a spirit of gentleness. Look to yourself, lest you too be tempted" (Gal. 6:1). Those who are called "spiritual" here are like physicians who must carefully choose a suitable medicine. The penalty imposed should be stern enough to help the offender realize the seriousness of his misbehavior. But you who are responsible for imposing this penalty should act in such a merciful way that, if you were guilty of the same fault, you would be willing to undergo the same punishment.[5]

9. Some persons, when they are guilty of any fault, conceal it, defend it, or minimize it. The sinful infection remains in them, however, even if its visible effects are few. This presents a serious problem to the director. He may recognize the signs that venom and rottenness have gathered in that part of the body even if there has been no outward eruption. He needs an opportunity to employ public correction to lance the infection, yet has no public evidence to go on so long as the guilty ones are unwilling to confess. If he rebukes the guilty, it does no good: he will have condemned sins but not corrected sinners. If he condones what he knows is going on, he burns with anxiety for his brother's soul, and, since he did nothing about the delinquency, for his own as well.

When no better course of action offers itself, a leader is well advised to wait, exercising patience and ignoring the sins that he cannot yet correct. Meanwhile, he should devote himself to prayer, a labor that may earn the conversion which his arguments cannot bring about. Perhaps at last, God will correct the individual quickly or uncover his concealed malice so that some remedy can finally be provided for it.

In the same way, our Lord silently tolerated the thief Judas for a long time and did not openly blame him until his wickedness increased so far that it broke out of itself into view. Even though Judas was morally sick unto death, as long as his sin remained hidden it did no harm to the souls of the rest, and so it was not blameworthy to tolerate it in silence. "Let both [the weeds and the wheat] grow together until the harvest" (Matt. 13:30). "Let the evildoer still do evil, and the filthy still be filthy" (Rev. 22:10).

The leader should, however, warn the whole community whenever he can to beware of occasions of sin, so as to awaken them to their danger. We read in Scripture, "Woe to that man by whom the Son of Man is betrayed" (Matt. 26:24). Yet Judas could not have

---

[5]The author is concerned here with faults that are known—and not just suspected—to the head and to other members of the community. In the next section, he makes it clear that a superior may not give public exposure to a brother's or sister's secret faults nor assign a penalty where wrongdoing is only suspected and not proved.

committed such a terrible offense so suddenly if he had not been lapsing, little by little, into an ever worse spiritual state. So it is plain that the Lord had long been quietly putting up with his evil condition: "Have I not held my peace, even for a long time?" (Isa. 57:11). For a guide to live and act justly, confronted by the difficulties that are brought on by the hidden sins of his brethren, demands great good judgment.

10. A third group of community members commit serious publicly known faults and refuse to accept appropriate correction. Sometimes they pretend to accept the correction but do not actually improve their conduct. This is harmful to other members of the community; either they are scandalized or, seeing that the guilty are not penalized for their offenses, begin to imitate them. They expect to be spared, as they have seen others spared, even a mild correction of their wrongdoing.

A director must, therefore, consider the expulsion of an offending member if four conditions come together: the wrongdoing is serious; the offense is public; the individual's long and habitual obstinacy in wrongdoing gives one no good reason to hope that he will ever accept correction; others are being infected by his example, or scandalized by tolerance of such conduct.

If all four conditions exist, what remains but to cast the dead sheep out of the flock, to cut off the gangrenous limb? Otherwise, those who are still healthy may also be infected and corrupted. "Drive out the wicked person from among you" (1Cor. 5:13). When someone wants to abandon his or her commitments and depart from the community, let that person go; indeed it is best that those who would create disturbances cut themselves off from the body. In the parable of the fig tree, our Lord represents the patience of God, who waits from year to year for the tree to bear fruit. But the time comes at last to cut down the unfruitful tree so that it may no longer burden the ground (Luke 13:6-9). "Even now the axe is laid to the root of the trees; every tree therefore that does not bear good fruit is cut down and thrown into the fire" (Matt. 32:19).

There should, of course, be no use of physical force in such an expulsion. Let mature and prudent persons who have the gift of good counsel from the Spirit of God advise the offending member and get him or her to agree to leave. "Do nothing without deliberation, and when you have acted, do not regret it" (Sir. 32:19).

To understand how much harm can come from the scandal given when a member of a Christian community lives an obviously sinful life, doing little good for anyone, consider the words of our Lord: "Whoever causes one of these little ones who believe in me to sin, it would be better for him to have a great millstone fastened round his neck and to be drowned in the depth of the sea" (Matt. 18:6). Let the offenders be put out, where they can do the worst harm chiefly to themselves, rather than allow them to contaminate the community.

Caring for Administrative Duties

11. Administration, along with works of service, constitutes the third type of work for which a head is responsible. In this regard he should commit some tasks to others and reserve some to himself. As much as possible, however, he should avoid and excuse himself from any superfluous duties. Thus Christ put his disciples, including Judas, in charge of obtaining the material necessities of life, while he personally retained the duty of preaching and healing. But when he was asked to divide an inheritance among several heirs, he answered, "Man, who made me a judge or divider over you?" (Luke 12:13-14).

12. A good leader delegates purely administrative responsibilities to others as much as possible. The ordinary necessities of life must indeed be taken care of, but a leader who takes charge of them himself risks losing sight of the more important, nobler part of his job. In his mind's eye he will tend to see less of the interior realities that are more necessary for salvation.

We see this in Scripture: "Choose able men from all the people, such as fear God, men who are trustworthy and who hate a bribe" (Exod. 18:19-22). "And let them judge the people at all times; every great matter they shall bring to you, but any small matter they shall decide themselves; so it will be easier for you, and they will bear the burden with you. It is not right that we should give up preaching the word of God to serve tables. Therefore, brethren, pick out from among you seven men of good repute, full of the Spirit and of wisdom, whom we may appoint to this duty. But we will devote ourselves to prayer and to the ministry of the word" (Acts 6:2-4).

There are some leaders who find it easier to delegate pastoral responsibilities than administrative work; this is a very serious error. If the head has no one to whom he can safely commit his temporal duties, it is better that he even risk being defrauded in these matters rather than devote his own attention to them. Christ has given an example of this; knowing that Judas was a thief, he still allowed him to make the purchases for the whole group of disciples. "He was a thief, and as he had the money box he used to take what was put into it" (John 12:6). Some leaders are personally involved in the management of community property, but far too quick to delegate the responsibility for spiritual guidance. It is an incomparably greater loss to endanger souls than to lose material possessions.

13. A leader should take personal responsibility for the spiritual concerns of the community. As their pastor and the guardian of their souls he ought to devote his energy chiefly to the things that pertain to spiritual progress and eternal salvation. These matters are at the heart of the shepherd's office.

These especially are the concerns for which a leader will render account before God's judgment seat:

- The leader preserves discipline within the community, so that the kind of life to which all are committed is maintained.
- He sees to it that the community lives together in peace and love.
- He should know the moral condition of every individual in the community and help each person resolve any difficulties.
- He should foresee and take action against the dangers into which his brethren may be led by their sins.
- He warns the members to improve their conduct; he throws light on doubtful issues and problematic decisions and corrects what must be corrected.
- He gives each member suitable formation for his work, so that everyone can do what he should for the whole

community, and do it correctly, without involving himself in any wrongdoing.

But when men cannot be satisfied except by offending God, we owe God our obedience; we owe only patience to men who misunderstand or find fault. "We must obey God rather than men" (Acts 5:29).

If we regard the community as a body, the one in charge is like the head. While the other members perform the actions appropriate to them, the head, being in charge of the whole, makes suitable provision for all. The head guides all the members, since all the senses—sight, hearing, touch, and so on—provide it with the necessary knowledge. The directions a leader gives, enforcing and relaxing the rules of the community, are like the coordinating functions of the body's nervous system.

The bodily head is not confined to any single specific activity, so that it can take care of the needs of all the members. It is better for every part of the body that the head hears, smells, tastes, and speaks for them all. The leader of a community serves the members in a similar way: "Obey your leaders and submit to them; for they are keeping watch over your souls, as men who will have to give account. Let them do this joyfully, and not sadly, for that would be of no advantage to you" (Heb. 13:17).

14. The best way to handle superfluous property, and business affairs that have no direct connection to the salvation or spiritual progress of souls, is to eliminate them. So far as possible, neither the head nor the members of the community should have anything to do with such matters. The time we have to serve the Lord is short; "let the day's own trouble be sufficient for the day" (Matt. 6:34). We have scarcely enough resources to take care of all that is needful. If we spend ourselves on pointless tasks or on things alien to our kind of life, we thereby neglect the more useful and better things. When we distract ourselves, applying our energies to many different projects, we become less able to concentrate on the specific duties that are most essential.[6]

---

[6]St. Gregory the Great gives the same teaching: "When the spirit is divided among many things, it is less able to deal with each one" (*Dialogues* I, ch. 4, see also *Pastoral Rule* I, 4).

For this reason, both the head and the members of a community should avoid preoccupations and excessive involvements with buildings, studies, legal actions, and other matters; these things are foreign to our call and we live more fruitfully without them.[7] When we are taken up with them, not only do we neglect better things, but very often we fall into wrongdoing. The use of exterior things reduces the mind's ability to perceive spiritual and interior realities, so that our desire for supernatural life grows lukewarm. When the body suffers a wound, infections that set in at the site of the injury must be treated at once to prevent the development of ulcers or tumors; so too, those who let themselves become wholly taken up by distracting business affairs, which are like untreated and infected wounds, promotes their own spiritual extinction.

The wise leader, therefore, ought to foresee the probable consequences of every project and set careful limits both on the business affairs that he lets the community take up and on the degree of involvement in such affairs that he permits. No more should be allowed than is clearly beneficial to the life of the community. "My son, do not busy yourself with many matters; if you multiply activities you will not go unpunished, and if you pursue you will not overtake, and by fleeing you will not escape" (Sir. 11:10). He is a careless steward in the Lord's house who, when he already bears a heavy load in his proper work, takes on several extra burdens that he could well do without.

Governing Oneself

15. Most important of all, a director ought to guard his own spiritual life, lest while he provides for others he should neglect himself or while helping others to find salvation he should submerge himself in danger (Matt. 16:26). "For what will it profit a man, if he gains the whole world and forfeits his life? Look to yourselves, that you may not lose what you have worked for, but

---

[7]The author here condemns commitment of time and energy to matters that can only distract individuals or the community from the primary religious commitments to personal conversion, worship, common life, apostolate, and Christian service. This does not forbid all involvement in social projects, secular careers, or cultural pursuits. The author is concerned only to condemn any patterns of the life of the individual or the community that would dissipate energies and multiply projects unnecessarily.

may win a full reward" (2John 8). This is the fourth level of the director's responsibilities, and it calls for self-examination in three areas.

16. The first aspect of good judgment concerning oneself regards the peace of one's own conscience. A leader ought to be able to say, in examining his conscience, that his actions are honorable and his motives pure. For the security of his conscience, he should not desire, do, order, or allow anything contrary to his commitments in the community, anything that violates decency and law, nor anything involving sin or scandal. If his conscience is to be clean, he must be sure that he never does or encourages good deeds for the sake of any human glory or self-gratification, but only to please God. Whatever a head does for God, as one who acts in his name, he should also do for God's sake, out of love for him. "If your eye is sound, your whole body will be full of light" (Matt. 6:22). That is, if love purifies the intention with which you act—which is the "eye" or focus of the activity—then the whole "body" of the action will earn the reward of eternal light. "But if your eye is not sound, your whole body will be full of darkness" (Matt. 6:23).

The leader should therefore study his conscience exactingly; with care he should determine what he has done, where he has failed, and what his real goals were in doing good. When he has examined his conscience he ought to repent of any evils he has discovered, confess them and correct them. If he sees that he has done good, he should take care to glorify the Lord for it and not himself (1Cor. 1:31). Like Christ, his master, he vigilantly cleanses the feet of others; but he cannot enter the Lord's house unless he cleanses his own. "Physician, heal yourself" (Luke 4:23).

When a leader thinks of the good he has done, he can rejoice without growing proud if he bears this consideration in mind: it was not for his own sake, but on behalf of those for whom he is responsible, that God has granted him the power to understand correctly, to speak well, or to do good.

17. The second aspect of the conduct of a leader that demands good judgment is his behavior and speech when he is engaged in serving others rather than himself. As one whose life is devoted to other people, he must always give a good example, meeting the needs of each person while pleasing all. His task is complex and

requires that he maintain a golden mean, eating neither too much nor too little, being neither immoderately gloomy nor jolly, weighty nor superficial, solitary nor social, silent nor a chatterer. He should speak without flattery or excessive harshness, and ought to be neither unreasonably strict nor slack in enforcing the rule. He should not avoid meeting with the community's guests, nor spend too much time with them. We should neither keep a suspicious watch on the activities of the brothers nor disregard them; should show neither favoritism nor prejudice.

It is, of course, impossible always to maintain the perfect balance, and so the course that consistently achieves the best results is to be as kind as possible. Kindness leads the members of the community to love their head better, obey him more willingly, turn to him more promptly with their problems, and follow his lead more quickly. His authority in the community is enough to make them fear him. If he is harsh and austere in addition, timid brothers will find his headship a heavy burden. "The weak you have not strengthened, the sick you have not healed, the crippled you have not bound up, the strayed you have not brought back, the lost you have not sought, and with force and harshness you have ruled them. So they were scattered, because there was no shepherd; and they became food for all the wild beasts" (Ezek. 34:4-5). "Do not be like a lion in your home, nor be a faultfinder with your servants" (Sir. 4:30).

For this reason, the chief of all shepherds, Our Lord Jesus, showed his love to us with much kindness, so that we would love and follow him. Our love for him as a man then drew us to know and love his divinity, "so that, while we come to know God in visible form, we are drawn by him to the love of his invisible nature.[8]

For the same reason, the leader of a community, as Christ's representative, ought to do his best to earn the willing love of those in his charge, so that he can more readily draw them to the love of Christ. In every doubtful case he should incline more to whatever choices will truly do the most for humility and charity, and to whatever decisions fit in best with pure gospel virtue.

---

[8] Preface for the Christmas season, Roman Missal.

18. Finally, a leader must use discretion in trusting his own good judgment. Unlike the bodily eye, which sees everything except itself, the wisdom which makes all judgments about everything for a community's life must not fail to judge itself as well. Otherwise, the leader will "think of himself more highly than he ought" (Rom. 12:3) and become one of "those who are wise in their own eyes, and shrewd in their own sight!" (Isa. 5:21, see also Rom. 11:25). Gregory the Great has observed, "the temptation of members of the community is to condemn the leader for every single mistake he may make. Likewise leaders are tempted to consider themselves wiser than the rest."[9] "Do you see a man who is wise in his own eyes? There is more hope for a fool than for him" (Prov. 26:12). For a foolish man, not trusting himself, will avoid deception by seeking wise men's advice. But a person who has too much confidence in his own ability often thinks he is right even when he is wrong!

Of all temptations, that which seems most dangerous for any Christian is to think too highly of his or her own opinion. For no one can be found, no matter how perceptive, who never falls into error. Those who regard their own view as wholly and exclusively right leave themselves open to any enemy clever enough to make a bad project seem attractive. The devil is most eager to worm his way in where he recognizes that people are trying to live virtuously; he wants to seek out the innocent man and destroy him just where he was hoping to give himself to God's service. "He sits in ambush in the villages; in hiding places he murders the innocent" (Ps. 10:8). The director, therefore, should take care to listen willingly to advice, and to seek it humbly.

19. There is a threefold value to seeking advice. First, when others agree with the leader's decision, he can be more confident that he has made no mistake. Then again, if something should go wrong, even though he followed the advice he received, he will not be wholly to blame as he would be had he acted completely on his own. Finally, when he humbly seeks advice, God often grants him an understanding that he lacked before. This may come from another's counsel or from his own thinking.

---

[9] *Moral Reflections on Job* XXXIV, c. 23, n. 50.

Thus Moses, who spoke face to face with God (Exod. 33:11), sought advice from Jethro, his father-in-law, and found it helpful (Exod. 18:18). Thus too the apostle Paul, a man who was filled with the Holy Spirit and who had received the Gospel message from a revelation by Jesus Christ, was prompted by the same Jesus to go to Jerusalem and discuss his preaching with Peter, James, and John so that he could make sure that his message did not differ from theirs (Gal. 2:1-10). In doing so he gave an example to faithful leaders, that they too should seek advice. "A man of judgment will not overlook an idea. . . . Do nothing without deliberation; and when you have acted, do not regret it" (Sir. 32:18-19).

Some men, however, when promoted to a governing position, imagine that they are continually filled with the spirit of knowledge, and that all the actions of their predecessors were stupid and perverse. Others, once they leave such a position, begin to condemn whatever their successors do. They pay no attention to the fact that, as they despised the actions of others, so the new leaders may despise theirs. "Woe to you! . . . when you have ceased to destroy, you will be destroyed" (Isa. 33:1). The person who judged the actions of others severely will find that others watch what he does very carefully indeed; they look for the faults in his conduct that he always found in others.

20. A prudent guide should be reluctant to take advice from either flatterers or slanderers. Flatterers will fool him into thinking more of himself than is good. They assure him that he is blessed in order to keep him from the truth about himself, when humility would have given him real self-knowledge (Isa. 3:12). Slanderers lead a person to suspect others of worse conduct than is true; often they bring about the condemnation of innocent people, or at least a wrong decision, before the truth is fully known. "Often many of those who are set in places of authority have been made in part responsible for the shedding of innocent blood, and have been involved in irremediable calamities, by the persuasion of friends who have been entrusted with the administration of public affairs, when these men by the false trickery of their evil natures beguile the sincere good will of their sovereigns" (Est. 16:5-6).

There are three common situations in which one ought to seek advice. When there is a question of improving the life of the community, one should consult with those most prudent in judgment, in order to settle any doubts about the right course of action. When it is necessary to back up a decision by showing that a strong authority supports it, one should consult persons of deserved prominence. If a consultation is held to ensure the community's peace and prevent any members from having occasion for murmuring at a decision, then all who are directly concerned in the decision should be consulted.

There are, however, innumerable special situations where good judgment is necessary. One cannot, therefore, give absolute rules about when and from whom to seek advice.

Chapter Seven

Devotion to God

1. Devotion to God is the sixth virtue of Christian leadership—the last, yet the most necessary, for all the other virtues depend on it. Love for God gives us zeal for good deeds, strengthens our patience, and clarifies our judgment. It is the foundation of all good example and the motive for brotherly compassion. Love of God is a spiritual anointing that teaches us everything that leads to salvation. "The anointing which you received [from the Holy Spirit] abides in you, and you have no need that anyone should teach you; as his anointing teaches you about everything" (1John 2:27).

2. Thus we see that devotion to God sheds light on our decisions: "The Counselor, the Holy Spirit, whom the Father will send in my name, he will teach you all things, and bring to your remembrance all that I have said to you" (John 14:26). It fires us with longing for the good: "Those who eat me will hunger for more, and those who drink me will thirst for more" (Sir. 24:21). It gives us strength to go on to perfection: "for God is at work in you both to will and to work for his good pleasure" (Phil. 2:13). It makes us disgusted with sin: "I hate and abhor falsehood, but I love thy law" (Ps. 119:163). It makes us act virtuously.

Devotion to God makes us act according to our words: "Be consistent in your thoughts; steadfast be your words" (Sir. 5:12). It gives a sweet savor to the knowledge that comes from faith: "For the wisdom of doctrine is according to her name" (Sir. 6:23).[1] It gives us hope and confidence in God: "It is the Spirit himself bearing witness with our spirit that we are children of God"(Rom. 8:16). And devotion to God itself grows within us, so that we love God the more: "God's love has been poured into our hearts through the Holy Spirit which has been given to us" (Rom. 5:5).

---

[1] In Latin, the word for "wisdom" is *sapientia*, which the author connects with *sapida*, "tasteful," and *scientia*, "knowledge." Therefore he asserts that the term "wisdom" means "tasteful knowledge," i.e. the believer has an appetite for wise and doctrinally sound teaching.

Devotion enables us to have a close personal relationship with God: "The Lord used to speak to Moses face to face, as a man speaks to his friend" (Exod. 33:11). Our prayers of petition grow more confident: "We have confidence before God, and we receive from him whatever we ask" (1John 3:21-22). And those prayers attain a new anointing and strength: "May he remember all your offerings, and regard with favor your burnt sacrifices" (Ps. 20:3).

Those who are filled with love of God become more loving themselves, for the spirit of wisdom is "beneficent, humane, steadfast" (Wis. 7:23). Their hearts grow humble: "I will look to the man that is humble and contrite in spirit" (Isa. 66:2). Their spirits are as lively as oil bubbling in a pan. They stand firm in the face of adversity: "The Lord is my light and my salvation; whom shall I fear?" (Ps. 27:1). They delight in every kind of good work; their love of wisdom is such that "companionship with her has no bitterness, and life with her has no pain, but gladness and joy" (Wis. 8:16). They set their minds on the things above: "If then you have been raised with Christ, seek the things that are above, where Christ is" (Col. 3:1).[2] They see the baseness of worldly concerns: "I have seen everything that is done under the sun; and behold, all is vanity and a striving after wind" (Eccles. 1:14). And so they long most for heaven: "My desire is to depart and to be with Christ" (Phil. 1:23).

Love of God wipes out our sins and the punishment due them: "Her sins, which are many, are forgiven for she loved much; but he who is forgiven little, loves little" (Luke 7:47). It increases the merit of our good deeds: "What is richer than wisdom who effects all things?" (Wis. 8:5). It helps us build up our neighbor's faith: "Incense and a pleasing odor as a memorial portion. We are the aroma of Christ to God" (Sir. 45:16).[3] Because we love God, demons flee from us: "Resist the devil and he will flee from you" (Jam.

---

[2]The author actually refers to Job 34:14 here, which in the Vulgate reads, "If he turns his heart to him, he shall draw his breath and spirit to himself." Modern scholarship has shown the Vulgate to be in error here, and so we have substituted a passage that better substantiates the author's point.

[3]The author imagines the virtues of a Christian as like odors attractive enough to draw others to the Lord.

4:7).[4] But the angels become our companions: "When you and your daughter-in-law Sarah prayed, I [the angel Raphael is speaking] ... was likewise present with you" (Tob. 12:12).

3. The grace of devout love for God confers all these benefits and many more, and so Christian leaders should be especially eager to have it. Their love for God will keep them always informed of what to do, help them do it, and head them off from wrong directions. Guides must pray not for themselves alone, but also for the people committed to their charge. They can care for others properly only with divine help: "Unless the Lord builds the house, those who build it labor in vain" (Ps. 127:1).

The leader of a community serves both God and those whom he leads; he is a mediator between them. He serves God by teaching God's people, correcting them, and by all the good he does. He serves people by pleading in prayer for their intentions and concerns and for their protection from all harm: "I stood between the Lord and you at that time" (Deut. 5:5).

4. We express devout love of God in three ways: public prayers in common with the whole community; private, personal prayer; and our constant awareness of God's presence in our daily lives.

Public Prayer

When the whole community worships God together, it should show devotion in its order, vigor, and fervor. Every public religious service should be orderly and free from confusion, carelessness, and delay, with each person fulfilling his responsibilities properly. "All things should be done decently and in order" (1Cor. 14:40). "David and the chiefs of the service also set apart for the service, [those] ... who should prophesy with lyres, with harps, and with cymbals" (1Chron. 25:1).

Since public worship is ministry to the Lord, we should take our part in it with vigor and a willing heart, not slothfully: "Cursed is he who does the work of the Lord with slackness" (Jer. 48:10). The whole service should be conducted with devout reverence, giving

---

[4] Another substitution for the Vulgate. The author's original reference was Tobit 6:8, which in the Vulgate reads "The smoke thereof driveth away all kinds of demons."

full attention to each part. Prayers should be spoken or sung in a voice neither crashingly loud nor spiritlessly soft. After all, we are praying in the sight of the angels and in the presence of God: "Sing praise with all your heart and voice, and bless the name of the Lord" (Sir. 39:35).

5. There are five reasons why the Spirit inspires the Christian people to celebrate public worship.

First, to imitate the heavenly choir, where saints and angels constantly sing God's praises in his very presence: "Blessed are those who dwell in thy house, ever singing thy praise" (Ps. 84:4). According to Christ's own promise—"I am with you always, to the close of the age" (Matt. 28:20)—we have him truly present with us, both by his Spirit and in the Eucharist. He deserves all our honor and praise, and we ought to show him whatever reverence we can. Unlike the singers in heaven, we cannot maintain uninterrupted praise. But we can at least assist in worship to the fullest degree our weakness permits. By so giving ourselves to the praise of God, we imitate the Jerusalem above, our mother (Gal. 4:26).

6. Second, we give thanks to God by offering prayers and praise at specific times that commemorate his loving deeds on our behalf.[5] Christ was born of the Virgin Mary at night; in the morning, before his passion, he came before his judge. He also rose from the dead very early in the morning. He was scourged at about nine in the morning; this was also the hour at which he sent the Holy Spirit upon the apostles. Noon was the hour of the crucifixion; at three in the afternoon he died for us. In the evening, at supper, he gave us the sacrament of his body and blood.

When we celebrate the Mass, we commemorate the Lord's passion. The Mass also brings us the grace of his presence and, under the form of the sacrament, provides the spiritual food of his body and blood. These are things we should never forget, and so we commemorate them at specified times. "I will recount the steadfast love of the Lord, the praises of the Lord, according to all that the Lord has granted us" (Isa. 63:7).

7. Third, public worship stirs up our devotion and fuels the fire of our love of God. Otherwise our idleness or the distraction of other activities will cause our love to grow cold. The priests of the

---

[5]The author here refers to the official hours of prayer in the monasteries.

Old Testament kept a fire constantly burning on the altar of the Temple, adding wood to it every morning (Lev. 4:12-13). For us Christians, that fire is the fervor of devotion, which should always burn on the altars of our hearts. Like the priest of the Temple, a leader whose life is consecrated to God's service should always nourish the fire of his love for God by heaping on it the wood of the divine praises. "I will bless the Lord at all times; his praise shall continually be in my mouth" (Ps. 34:1).

8. Fourth, public worship is of special benefit to immature or weak Christians who have trouble establishing a regular prayer life. When the whole community observes regular times of worship, these Christians grow accustomed to a well-defined life of prayer. They at least come to church to pray when the rest of the community gathers there. Moreover, they will be more likely to persevere in prayer if they can observe and take part in the community celebration of the acts of God. The liturgical services of the Jewish priesthood had this function: "The whole multitude of the people were praying outside at the hour of incense" (Luke 1:10).

The fact is that many poorly taught Christians hardly ever spend time in personal prayer. It is all the more important that they be called into church at definite times to celebrate the saving acts of God and to hear the word of God. Then they may develop the habit of worship.

9. Fifth, even non-Christians and heretics gather together regularly for public worship. However mistaken their beliefs, their faithfulness to worship should be an example to us. We who know the truths of Christianity have even greater reason to worship than they, so it is fitting that our worship be orderly and beautiful. We should come together both frequently and solemnly to praise our Creator and to celebrate the true and holy mysteries of our faith. Such worship brings us grace and prepares us for eternal life. Services that are both solemn and fervent also attract ordinary Christians to a love and reverence for religious things. David "gave beauty to the feasts and arranged their times throughout the year, while they praised God's holy name, and the sanctuary resounded from early morning" (Sir. 47:9-10).

Of all the external observances of worship, we ought to give the greatest attention to the public celebration of the Divine

Office, conducting it in an orderly, vigorous, and devout manner, as has been said before. At other times we are doing things for God, but here we stand before him, hearing and speaking to him; here we are able to beg him for help in our own necessities.

Private Prayer

10. Private prayer must also have a place in a Christian leader's life. He should be familiar with the psalms, litanies, and other vocal prayers so that he can recite them reflectively, choosing those that have the deepest meaning for him at a particular time. Our Savior recommended the Lord's Prayer as a vocal prayer: "When you pray, say "Our Father. . . " (Luke 11:2; Matt. 6:9).

A leader should also spend time meditating on sacred things. He should bring before his mind's eye his own sins and shortcomings; he should reflect on future plans or on the benefits granted by God. He should consider Christ's passion, his goodness, and the rewards promised to his followers. Meditation on such subjects should lead to devout feelings of reverent love for God, of desire for him, and of sorrow for sin or joy in salvation. "I commune with my heart in the night; I meditate and search my spirit" (Ps. 77:6).

Feelings of personal attachment to God are of great importance. At times, one experiences tears or sighs or other indescribable movements of the heart: "The Spirit himself intercedes for us with sighs too deep for words" (Rom. 8:26). One also feels a great sense of love, internal jubilations, intense rejoicing and rapture, and absorption of one's whole spirit in God: "He who is united to the Lord becomes one spirit with him" (1Cor. 6:17). Such unity starts with a purification of our understanding that allows us to know God himself. That personal knowledge results in an ardent love for God which is so fulfilling that it binds us inseparably to him.

11. The leader's many responsibilities often distract him and get in the way of his devotional life. When that happens he should at least take any brief opportunities he gets—as it were, secretly and by stealth—to restore himself to zealous prayer. No one should be so busy that he allows his fervor to grow completely cold, stops all prayer, drifts away from a personal relationship

with God, and little by little abandons the grace given him, thus ceasing to please God. Moses, although taken up by duties to the people, often turned back to the Lord in the tent of the covenant. There he spoke personally with the Lord, finding in God refreshment for his spirit. Our Lord also, while preaching to the crowd by day, spent his nights in solitary prayer.

The head of a community may get few chances to spend a long time praying. But he is certainly given, at times, a greater grace of praying for others, since that is his duty. And it is right that those he is serving should have the benefit of his prayers. When he does have a chance to devote himself to prayer, he ought to make good use of it. He should try his best to find such chances, for if he ignores them, his ingratitude will deprive him of grace.

Awareness of God's Presence

12. The leader, like anyone else who desires to grow spiritually by sharing his life with other Christians, ought to be constant in his devotion to God. Such constancy takes three forms.

First, he should remain internally aware of God's yoke—the task and the grace that he has given to us. "I keep the Lord always before me. My eyes are ever toward the Lord" (Ps. 16:8; 25:15). Always and everywhere, a person should aim to live as if God were visibly present. So Elijah and Elisha used to say: "As the Lord of hosts lives, before whom I stand" (1Kings 18:15; see also 1Kings 17:1, 2Kings 3:14). Such alertness requires that we turn our minds fully and decisively to the Lord.

The angels, wherever they may be sent, never stop gazing upon God. In the same way a virtuous person, as much as he can, always keeps the memory of God in his heart. If at times he fails in this, he should rebuke himself. Bernard of Clairvaux says, "Think of the time as lost when you have not been aware of God."[6]

Of course we cannot continually concentrate on the Lord in profound meditation; but at least we should remember his presence and direct the gaze of our hearts towards him. When sculptors obtain the material for a statue, they study it from every angle; then, when an opportunity comes, they are ready to give it the

---

[6] *Meditations*, Chapter 6, n. 18.

proper shape. So too, mindfulness of God will be shaped into meditation or prayer when the opportunity comes.

13. The leader should also maintain a constant determination to please God in every speech and action. This leads us to take as much care not to displease or grieve him as we would in his visible presence. Instead, we strive to make our deeds and our ways of doing things more pleasing to him: "Whether we are at home or away, we make it our aim to please him" (2Cor. 5:9).

A person who has committed himself to the Christian life should always act as though he were about to appear before the judgment seat of the Most High: "You also must be ready; for the Son of Man is coming at an hour you do not expect" (Luke 12:40). The Lord sees all of our actions; he does not forget our good deeds, but rewards them in due time. Neither will he neglect to punish our wrongdoing, if we do not do penance. "A man who breaks his marriage vows says to himself, 'Who sees me? Darkness surrounds me, and the walls hide me, and no one sees me. Why should I fear? The Most High will not take notice of my sins.' His fear is confined to the eyes of men, and he does not realize that the eyes of the Lord are ten thousand times brighter than the sun; they look upon all the ways of men, and perceive even the hidden places"(Sir. 23:18-19).

14. Finally, a leader should prepare for everything he does with prayer, at least mentally. Whatever the circumstances, one can arm oneself with prayer and offer thanks and praise to God for all his goodness. A leader asks the Lord to inspire him with worthwhile plans for his work, to direct his projects so that they help people reach salvation, and to preserve and increase the good done.

When a sailor can tell that a storm is coming, he usually makes haste to get to a safe port. In the same way, committed Christians regularly turn to the harbor of prayer, where they can escape from all the conflicts that endanger them. In all of their duties they should put more confidence in prayer than in their own activity and labor: "O Our God, wilt thou not execute judgment upon them? For we are powerless against this great multitude that is coming against us. We do not know what to do, but our eyes are upon thee" (2Chron 20:12). "As the eyes of servants look to the hand of their master, as the eyes of a maid to the hand of her mistress, so our eyes look to the Lord our God, till he have mercy on us" (Ps. 123:2).

15. The spiritual leader needs to have the qualities discussed above, and others as well, in order to do his service. He is like one of the seraphim in Isaiah's vision whose six wings lift on high, cover their bodies and their feet, and rise above their heads (Isa. 6:1-4). The character of a Christian leader is like the wings of the seraphim.

First, the leader is raised up and sustained by a right intention and by brotherly love. Thus desire for human praise will not infect his zeal, nor will personal preferences unbalance his compassion. The only reward he seeks is in heaven: "I have inclined my heart to do thy justifications forever; for the reward" (Ps. 119:112).

Next, patience and a life of good example protect him from the spiritual spears of troublemakers and cover the nakedness of lack of merits. These virtues are both defensive armor and sacred vestments. "Put on your strength, O Zion; put on your beautiful garments, O Jerusalem, the holy city" (Isa. 52:1).

Prudent good judgment helps a leader, wherever he goes, to see what he should do and how it should be done. And by zealous devotion to God he seeks "the things that are above, where Christ is, seated at the right hand of God" (Col. 3:1), coming into his presence as though he were borne aloft into that sublime height, his virtues being like wings to raise him.

It is not possible for all spiritual leaders to possess all these qualities equally. But it is absolutely necessary that each leader possess at least some degree of each virtue. This is just as important for the spiritual formation of those whom they direct as it is for their own salvation.

Every Christian with a real commitment to God ought to be adorned with these virtues; even if he has only his own soul to govern, he will at the end come before God's judgment seat to render an account for that. These virtues, therefore, should lift him up like wings and pinions: fervent righteousness, compassion on his neighbors for the sake of God, patience in adversities, good example that helps others grow spiritually, prudence in all things. Above all, every committed Christian clings to God, maintaining his personal relationship with his Father through zealous prayer, asking God to protect, direct, and guide him in all things, and at last to lead him up to heaven. May Jesus Christ mercifully grant this to us. Amen.

Translator's Note

The Latin text used in preparing this translation comes from the complete edition of Bonaventure's writings prepared by the Franciscans of the College of St. Bonaventure (Quarracchi: 1898). In a few places, the references to Scripture have been changed to account for differences between the Vulgate and modern editions of the Bible. I have also modified the author's use of the analogy of the six-winged Seraph.